簡単に作れる日本食

JAPANESE FOOD
MADE EASY

簡単に作れる日本食

JAPANESE FOOD MADE EASY

AYA NISHIMURA

murdoch books

Sydney | London

CONTENTS

INTRODUCTION

Japanese food has the reputation of being hard to make and taking years to master. Although this may be true for some specialist styles of cooking, food that is eaten at home in Japan is very simple and easy to cook and prepare. Furthermore, it is healthy and can be easily introduced into everyday cooking.

Most Japanese food can be made very quickly as long as you can get fresh ingredients and a few simple seasonings. The basic seasonings include soy sauce, miso, vinegar, sugar, salt, sake, dashi stock and mirin (Japanese food rarely uses spices). These eight flavours, used in different proportions and combined with fresh ingredients, are the essence of Japanese cooking.

This book will introduce you to many popular modern Japanese recipes, such as tonkatsu, ramen and gyoza. It also showcases Japanese recipes that are generally eaten at home – which are very easy to cook but rarely eaten in restaurants – dishes like grilled Padrón peppers with bonito flakes, kakiage fritters, homemade fried tofu and sesame tofu.

This book will teach you how to use healthy ingredients, such as miso and tofu, in everyday cooking – from traditional miso soup and miso-marinated fish to more Western-flavoured tofu and tomato salads, tofu cheesecakes and miso caramel sauce.

Learn how to make homemade teriyaki sauce, tonkatsu sauce, miso dressing, shichimi togarashi, furikake sprinkles – these useful seasonings can instantly give your cooking a Japanese flavour. They are all free from preservatives and much healthier than the ready-made seasonings from a shop.

There are, of course, instructions on how to make dashi stock from scratch or sashimi and sushi for those who would like to try making more traditional Japanese food.

Japanese food is simple. There is no need for difficult techniques or rare ingredients in home cooking. Well-selected ingredients and seasonings, use of texture and subtle attention to detail will lead to surprisingly delicious results, where a simple dish is elevated to something truly special. These are the secrets of Japanese cooking.

My heartfelt hope is that this book helps you to discover how simple, delicious and healthy Japanese food can be, and that it becomes part of your daily cooking and weekend gatherings with family and friends.

FOOD MAP OF JAPAN

01: HOKKAIDO

This is the second-largest island, with extensive natural resources and it is also famous for its ski resorts. Well-known dishes include miso butter ramen, sushi and seafood such as crab, sea urchins, scallops and salmon.

02: AKITA

This is the northern part of the Japanese Honshu mainland, famous for its *onsen* (hot spring bath). This area is known for high-quality rice, sake (many renowned sake brewers are from here), *kiritanpo nabe* (a special type of hotpot) and *inaniwa* udon noodles.

03: TOKYO

This is the capital of Japan and one of the biggest, most cosmopolitan cities in the world. It is the birthplace of nigiri sushi and known for *chanko nabe* (a hotpot traditionally eaten by sumo wrestlers).

04: SHIZUOKA

This city is famous for the Onsen area, which offers hot spring baths. It's well known for its eel cuisine, such as *unaju* (charcoal-grilled eels on rice) and wild/farmed eel, as well as tea production and fresh wasabi.

05: KYOTO

This city used to be the capital of Japan. It is well known for various types of pickles, such as *senmaizuke*, *shibazuke* and *suguki*, and fresh tofu and other tofu products, such as fried tofu and *ganmodoki*. Other dishes to note are *kappo ryori* (a traditional prix-fixe menu/fine dining style where the chef cooks right in front of you), *wagashi* (traditional Japanese sweets), *saba* (mackerel) sushi, and the especially famous *saikyo miso*, which is an extra-sweet white miso. It is also one of the biggest green tea farming districts.

06: OSAKA

This is an energetic, friendly city that is famous for its hearty street food. Its well-known dishes include *okonomiyaki* (savoury pancake) and *takoyaki* (octopus balls). Kushikatsu restaurants near Shinsekai are also worth noting.

07: HYOGO

This is a cosmopolitan port city. It is particularly renowned for its world-famous Kobe beef, *akashiyaki* (octopus balls with dashi broth) and its array of seafood, such as red sea bream, octopus and oysters.

08: KAGAWA

Located in Shikoku island, Kagawa is the smallest prefecture of Japan, but has a rich food culture. This area is known for sanuki-style udon. Udon noodle manufacturers have also opened casual canteen-style restaurants to the public to serve the freshest and cheapest udon noodles.

09: HIROSHIMA

This is the largest city in the western Honshu island. This area is known for Hiroshima-style *okonomiyaki* (savoury pancakes) and fresh oysters.

10: YAMAGUCHI

This area is famous for its *fugu* (puffer/blowfish) cuisine. This lethally poisonous fish is prepared by highly qualified chefs, who must obtain a licence to handle the fish. It is a luxurious Japanese delicacy.

11: FUKUOKA

This city has an area with countless street food stands and is well known for *tonkatsu ramen* (very rich pork broth ramen) and *karashi mentaiko* (salted sacks of cod roe with chilli).

12: OKINAWA

This is one of the main islands, but it is remote and tropical. Due to the climate and abundant produce, this area has a very specific food culture. Dishes of note are Okinawa soba noodle (pork belly and noodles) and *chanpuru* (Okinawa-style stir-fry, often cooked with bitter melon).

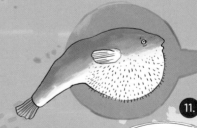

YAMAGUCHI
fugu *(puffer/blowfish)*
cuisine

FUKUOKA
tonkatsu ramen
(very rich pork broth ramen)

HOKKAIDO
sushi and seafood
01.

AKITA
kiritanpo nabe
*(a special type
of hotpot)*
02.

HIROSHIMA
Hiroshima-style
okonomiyaki *(savoury
pancakes)*
09.

HYOGO
Kobe beef

KYOTO
wagashi *(traditional
Japanese sweets)*

TOKYO
*birthplace of
nigiri sushi*
03.

05.

07.   06.

08.

SHIZUOKA
tea production
04.

KAGAWA
udon noodles

OSAKA
takoyaki *(octopus balls)*

OKINAWA
*Okinawa soba noodle
(pork belly and noodles)*
12.

N
W   E
S

FRESH INGREDIENTS

01. TOFU/BEAN CURD

Made from soybeans, tofu is known as a healthy food as it is high in protein and iron and low in calories. There are several varieties of tofu typically available. The soft (silken) tofu is eaten raw or in miso soup. The firm (cotton) tofu is best for frying. Thick deep-fried tofu is referred to as *atsuage*; thin deep-fried tofu is called *aburaage*. Deep-fried tofu freezes well and is a great meat substitute.

Once opened, tofu needs to be refrigerated. It should be covered with water and consumed within 1–2 days.

02. SPRING ONIONS

Spring onions (scallions) are common in Japanese cooking, most typically as a garnish. Spring onion is often finely sliced or shredded and sprinkled on the meal towards the end of cooking.

03. SHISO/PERILLA LEAF

This aromatic leaf comes from the same plant family as mint. There are green and red shiso leaves but the green ones are more widely available. Shiso leaves can be found in Japanese/Asian grocery stores. You will often find them packed in a plastic tray or in a bunch in the chilled section. The green shiso leaf is typically used as a herb in cold dishes and is also great for tempura. The red shiso leaf is often used when dyeing pickles red.

04. GINGER

Ginger is a very common ingredient in Japanese dishes. It is used in recipes for pickles, stews, sauces and dressings as well as sweets and puddings. It is often finely grated and used as a garnish. Ginger is also used to offset the strong odours of certain fish and meat. Try to use fresh-looking ginger rather than dried or older ginger.

A Japanese grater, called an *oroshiki* or *oroshigane*, is a useful tool. They are available in Japanese grocery stores or can be ordered online.

05. DAIKON RADISH

Daikon (also known as mooli) is an Asian radish that is long and white with green leaves. A raw daikon should have a fresh, crisp bite but once it is slow-cooked, it should become soft and sweet and almost melt in your mouth. It is eaten simmered or slow-cooked and can also be grated, mixed with a little soy sauce and served with rolled omelette or added to a dipping sauce.

When you grate daikon, use a fine microplane grater, the finest side of a cheese grater or a food processor (or an *oroshiki*, see above). The flesh needs to be puréed rather than shredded.

06. CHINESE/NAPA CABBAGE (WONG BOK)

This is an Asian variety of cabbage. It is elongated and has pale leaves and wide stems. The leaves and stems are softer than other types of cabbage, and usually taste fresh and sweet. It is often used in gyoza dumplings, soups, stews, stir-fry dishes and as a main component in hotpots.

07. SHIITAKE MUSHROOMS

Shiitakes are nutritious mushrooms that are high in vitamin B and minerals. Shiitake mushrooms add an umami flavour to dishes when used in either the fresh or dried form. Fresh shiitake mushrooms are used in simmered dishes or for tempura. Dried shiitake mushrooms must be soaked in water to rehydrate them. They are commonly used to make vegetarian dashi. Dried shiitake mushrooms can also be used in place of fresh shiitake mushrooms once rehydrated.

08. ENOKI, SHIMEJI, OYSTER AND KING OYSTER MUSHROOMS

There are many varieties of Japanese mushrooms that are widely available. They are all good to use in hotpots and soups. Enoki mushrooms are white in colour and have long, thin stems. They have a nice crunchy texture when you bite them. There are two kinds of shimeji; one is brown and the other is white. Oyster mushrooms and king oyster mushrooms are also often used in Japanese cooking.

09. LOTUS ROOT

Lotus root is actually a rhizome that is grown in muddy ponds. It has a woody look and a pale-yellow, speckled skin. The flesh has holes in it that make this vegetable very distinctive in appearance. The texture of the flesh is crunchy like a water chestnut. Lotus root is sold fresh as a whole vegetable in a vacuum-sealed package, or peeled, chopped and frozen in a bag. It is used to make pickles, in stews, in tempura or deep-fried and served as chips.

10. NASHI/ASIAN PEARS

Nashi pears are a variety of Asian pears. They look like a pale-yellow version of an apple. They are often eaten peeled and raw. Nashi have a high water content and fresh, crisp flesh, with an amazingly fragrant smell.

LIQUIDS

01. SOY SAUCE

Soy sauce is an essential component and one of the core seasoning elements in Japanese cuisine. It is made from fermented soybeans, wheat, salt, brine and koji, which is a mould culture that grows naturally on grain. The three major varieties of soy sauce are dark (*koikuchi*), light (*usukuchi*) and tamari.

Dark soy sauce is most commonly used in cooking and in sauces. Light soy sauce is lighter in colour, but it has a higher salt content. Therefore, it is used for seasoning clear broths and for dishes in which you want to retain the vibrant colour. Tamari does not contain wheat and is mainly used as a dipping sauce.

Chinese dark soy sauce is much darker in colour, has a more intense flavour and is not suitable for Japanese cooking. However, Chinese light soy sauce and commercial, supermarket-brand light soy sauces tend to have a similar consistency to Japanese dark ones and work well if you cannot find a Japanese brand, such as Kikkoman.

02. VINEGAR

This is another one of the important seasonings in Japanese cooking. Rice vinegar is made from fermented rice and has a mellow, sweet flavour. It is typically used for pickling, dressings and, most famously, for seasoning sushi rice. Again, try to use Japanese rice vinegar for Japanese cooking – Chinese rice vinegar tends to be a little more acidic. Mitsukan is the most widely available Japanese brand.

Rice vinegar is the most common, but there are also other types of vinegar used in Japanese cooking, such as brown rice vinegar and grain vinegar. There are also pre-mixed seasoned rice vinegars or *sushi-su*

(seasoned vinegar made especially for sushi) available, which are pre-mixed with sugar and salt. Be careful not to confuse these with pure vinegar since the flavour will be entirely different.

03. MIRIN

Mirin is a sweetened, fortified rice wine that's used for cooking and as a primary seasoning in Japanese cuisine. It has a subtle sweetness compared to sugar. It is made from glutinous rice, *kome koji* (a fermented rice) and brewed alcohol. Mirin that has been made traditionally includes no additional sugar. However, there are 'mirin-style seasonings' available that are made with additional sugar and a lower percentage of alcohol. These are usually much sweeter than traditional mirin.

Mirin adds a delicate, rounded sweetness and umami to your cooking. Also, its high sugar content allows it to act as a glaze.

Although mirin is sometimes called sweetened sake or rice wine, I wouldn't recommend drinking it. If your mirin runs out, you can substitute it with light brown sugar or white sugar, but use only one-third of the quantity.

04. SAKE

Sake is a traditional Japanese alcohol. Although it is sometimes called rice wine, sake is produced by a brewing process more similar to beer than wine. Sake adds a delicate sweetness, fragrance and depth of flavour to dishes.

There are cooking sakes available, but I would recommend using a cheaper drinking sake for cooking, similar to how you might use a red or white wine in Western cooking. Similarly, cooking concentrates the

flavour so starting with a sake that you would like to drink is preferable.

For drinking, there are many varieties of sake available. Some are meant to be served cold; others are served warm. Luckily, the availability of sake outside Japan has increased in recent years. I would suggest asking the store assistant for advice about possible pairings to go with your Japanese dishes.

05. TOASTED SESAME OIL

Toasted sesame oil is darker in colour than non-toasted oil and has a distinctively stronger flavour. Toasted sesame oil is rarely used as a cooking oil. Instead, it tends to be used for flavouring due to its lower smoking point and its robust flavour. Just a few drops added at the end of the cooking process can contribute a nutty flavour and a fantastic aroma to a dish.

06. YUZU JUICE

Yuzu is a small, Japanese citrus fruit. Only the skin and the juice are used in cooking and it is rarely eaten as a fruit. It has a delicate but powerful aroma and flavour. Unfortunately, the actual fruit is not widely available outside of Japan. Luckily, we can find bottles of yuzu juice in Japanese/Asian grocery stores. It's usually sold in a tiny bottle, but since the fruit has such a strong aroma and flavour, you only need a dash of the juice in a recipe; a little bit goes a long way.

PANTRY

01. KATSUOBUSHI (BONITO FLAKES)

Katsuobushi is dried, fermented and smoked skipjack tuna that is often sold in the form of shaved flakes in a plastic bag. This is one of the principal ingredients in dashi stock. It is also used to sprinkle on various dishes, such as *okonomiyaki* (savoury pancakes), salad, tofu and even on plain, steamed rice. It adds instant umami to dishes.

02. KOMBU (DRIED KELP)

Dried seaweed is another one of the main ingredients for dashi stock. It is also used for flavouring various dishes, such as pickles, and adds an umami flavour.

03. DRIED SHIITAKE

This umami-packed dried mushroom adds a strong earthy flavour that is very nourishing and is mainly used in basic and vegetarian dashi stock. It can also be added to stews, miso soup and many other dishes.

04. POWDERED DASHI/ DASHI PACKS

Surprisingly, good-quality powdered dashi is readily available, and this convenient shortcut is widely and commonly used in Japanese home cooking. Making dashi from scratch is worthwhile, but it isn't the quickest or even the cheapest option.

   The most common powdered dashi is sold in a box of small sachets. Dashi packs are like tea bags with whole ingredients, which offer very good flavour and convenience. I recommend choosing organic powdered dashi or

dashi packs to avoid any additives. Always follow the packet instructions for preparing the dashi.

05. SHICHIMI TOGARASHI

Although spice is uncommon in Japanese cooking, this spice mix is a staple at the Japanese dinner table. It simply means 'seven spices'. It is often used for hot broth-based noodle dishes or in a *donburi* (rice bowl) dish.

06. UMEBOSHI

Umeboshi is pickled *ume*, which is a Japanese plum/apricot. It is sold in the form of the whole pickled fruit or as a puréed paste in a jar or tube. Because of the extreme sourness and saltiness, it is often used as a garnish or condiment in very small amounts. After a jar of umeboshi is opened, it should be kept in the fridge.

07. PICKLED GINGER

Pickled ginger is chiefly served with sushi as a palate cleanser, but it is also great with tofu and as a salad topping. Traditionally, pickled ginger is made with fresh ginger when it is in season – this is called *shin shoga* (new ginger). It still has the pink buds attached, which naturally turn the ginger pink in the process of pickling. Nowadays, the ginger is usually coloured with red shiso leaves or coloured artificially. Once a packet of pickled ginger has been opened, it should be kept in the fridge.

08. NORI

Nori is used primarily for making sushi. It is also used to make *onigiri* rice balls and as a garnish on other dishes. It is sold as a pack of square sheets. However, there is also a flavoured nori that is sold in smaller packets with a small rectangular shape, which is fantastic for *onigiri* rice balls.

09. WAKAME

This dried seaweed is soaked in water to rehydrate it and is used in soups or for making salads. There are also other types of dried seaweed available, such as hijiki and arame.

10. AONORI POWDER

This is a dried and powdered form of green laver seaweed. It is used as a topping for *okonomiyaki* and can be sprinkled on food to add aroma.

11. SHORT-GRAIN RICE/ SUSHI RICE

This is a starchy rice and is stickier than most other rice varieties, which makes it easier to eat with chopsticks. There are plenty of rice brands and makers in Japan. It is worth trying different brands or types of rice, especially when the newly harvested rice (*shinmai*) is available.

Short-grain brown rice (*genmai*) is also available and is a healthier option. Just make sure you choose an organic variety since unpolished rice tends to retain more pesticides. Cooking brown rice requires extra soaking time due to the extra layer of bran.

12. UDON NOODLES

This thick, wheat-flour noodle is one of the most popular types of noodle, especially in the Kansai region. It is available dried, semi-fresh in packs or frozen. I would highly recommend using the frozen ones since they retain their amazing silky texture and have a nice bite. Plus, they are convenient as they cook in minutes.

13. SOBA NOODLES

Soba noodles are another popular type of noodle. This grey/light-brown, thin noodle is traditionally made from buckwheat flour. However, it can often be mixed with wheat flour, so check the packet if you prefer 100 per cent buckwheat soba noodles. Outside Japan, soba noodles are mostly sold in dried form.

PANTRY

14. PANKO BREADCRUMBS

These are Japanese-style breadcrumbs that are sharper and crispier and have a more delicate texture compared to regular breadcrumbs.

15. TONKATSU SAUCE

This is the Japanese version of Worcestershire sauce. It is called tonkatsu sauce because it is typically served with tonkatsu. *Okonomiyaki* and *yakisoba* sauces are sold in a very similar form and are almost identical in flavour, but *okonomiyaki* sauce is sweeter and *yakisoba* sauce is saltier. These are used for *okonomiyaki* (savoury pancakes) and *yakisoba* (fried noodles).

16. WASABI

Wasabi comes from the same plant family as horseradish and is similar in appearance. However, the wasabi stem colour is a lighter green. It has a strong, pungent mustardy flavour and is traditionally used as a condiment, especially with sushi. The fresh stem is hard to get outside Japan. However, it is widely available as a paste or in the powdered form. I would recommend using the paste for the best flavour. It keeps well in the fridge once it has been opened.

17. SUGAR

Sugar is frequently used in Japanese cooking. Light brown, granulated or caster (superfine) sugar are all regularly used. *Kurozato* (black sugar) is also used for traditional sweets, wagashi making and sugar syrups. The flavour of *kurozato* is similar to molasses, but it is made from cane sugar.

18. KATAKURIKO/ ARROWROOT FLOUR

This is a starch made from the katakuri plant (*Erythronium japonicum*) that is used as a thickening agent. You can replace it with cornflour (cornstarch), which works in the same way. However, I recommend using arrowroot for Homemade Sesame Tofu (see page 70).

19. GLUTINOUS/ SWEET RICE FLOUR

This produces a soft, pliable and elastic dough and is used to make *mochi* and other Asian baked goods.

20. SESAME SEEDS

These are available in white and black; the black ones have a stronger flavour. They are used for everyday Japanese cooking, as a garnish, in dressings and often in desserts.

21. NERIGOMA/ SESAME PASTE

This is very similar to tahini, but the most important difference is that *nerigoma* is made from unhulled sesame seeds and tahini is made from hulled sesame seeds. There is also a black sesame *nerigoma* available.

22. MATCHA POWDER/ GREEN TEA POWDER

Matcha is a finely ground powder made from green tea leaves specifically produced for this purpose. It is becoming very popular and was recently classified as a superfood. Matcha is widely used in traditional and modern Japanese sweets and puddings, and even in soba noodles.

Once opened, matcha should be properly sealed and refrigerated.

23. HOJICHA/ ROASTED GREEN TEA

This tea has a lovely toasty, slightly caramel flavour. The roasting process turns green tea leaves to brown leaves and lowers the level of caffeine in the tea. Because of the low caffeine content and also the lower price, *hojicha* (also called *bancha*) is more commonly consumed than green tea in Japan.

24. KINAKO/ROASTED SOYBEAN POWDER

Powdered roasted soybeans add an amazing nutty flavour. This is often used when making Japanese sweets.

MAGIC MISO

Miso is a traditional and principal Japanese condiment, which adds instant umami and depth of flavour to your cooking. It is a fermented soybean paste made with rice, barley or other grains, salt, water and a fermentation starter called koji (*Aspergillus oryzae*). Koji is a mould that is typically grown on steamed rice, beans or other grains. It is an important ingredient in the production of soy sauce and Japanese alcoholic beverages, such as sake and shochu.

Making miso is a well-respected craft in Japan and is the equivalent of wine or cheese making in Europe. There are thousands of traditional miso makers in Japan.

There are also countless varieties of miso in Japan, similar to the numerous types of cheese that are available in the West. The colours and texture, such as coarseness and smoothness, vary depending on the brand and the maker.

These variations are due to the differing lengths of the fermentation process as well as the use of a variety of ingredients. A longer fermentation process creates a more complex and robust flavour. If the fermentation process is shorter, the miso tends to be sweeter and milder in taste.

White miso is the most popular type of miso used in Japan; red miso is a close second and is also extremely common. These are versatile types of miso to use and are the most accessible in supermarkets in the West as well.

Miso needs to be kept refrigerated in a sealed container. It is traditionally sold unpasteurised and contains a number of valuable nutrients, microorganisms and enzymes, which can easily be destroyed if the miso becomes overheated. It should be added towards the end of making a miso soup or any other type of cooking process.

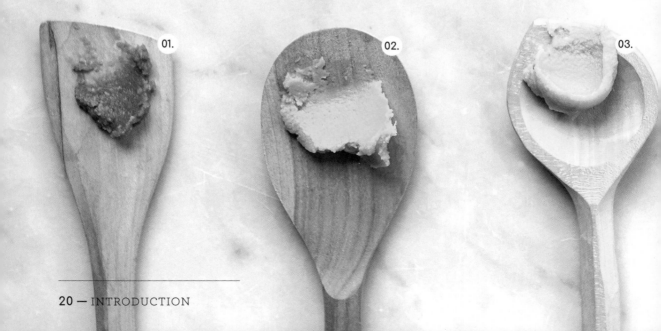

01. 02. 03.

01. AKA MISO/RED MISO

Main ingredients: rice and soybeans

Appearance: deep caramel colour to reddish brown

Flavour: aromatic and tangy, stronger in umami, slight caramel flavour

Suitable for: meat marinades and miso soup

Fermentation: over 12 months

Region: Northern and Kanto region

02. SHIRO/WHITE MISO

This is also sometimes called yellow miso or shinshu miso to distinguish it from the sweeter white miso.

Main ingredients: rice and soybeans

Appearance: actually not 'white' in colour, rather yellow to pale brown

Flavour: mild, gentle sweetness, with a slightly salty note

Suitable for: fish and vegetable marinades, soups and sauces

Fermentation: over 6 months

Region: Kansai region

03. SAIKYO/SWEET WHITE RICE MISO

Main ingredients: high percentage of rice and soybeans

Appearance: pale, beige in colour, very smooth, looser in consistency than the others

Flavour: delicate, sweet, gentle in saltiness, tastes almost like a custard

Suitable for: marinades, miso soup and sauces

Fermentation: 3 months

Region: Kyoto

04. MUGI/BARLEY MISO

Main ingredients: barley and soybeans

Appearance: dark brown and usually coarse in texture

Flavour: mild, sweet, malty

Suitable for: marinades, miso soup and stews

Fermentation: 2-3 years

Region: Kyushu, Shikoku, Western Chugoku area

05. HATCHO MISO

Main ingredients: only soybeans

Appearance: deep, dark brown, dense

Flavour: less sweet; salty, strong and chocolatey

Suitable for: sauces and stews

Fermentation: up to 3 years

Region: Aichi prefecture

06. GENMAI MISO/ BROWN RICE MISO

Main ingredients: brown rice and soybeans

Appearance: dark brown

Flavour: strong, chocolatey

Suitable for: miso soup, sauces, marinades and dressings

Fermentation: minimum of 2 years

There are also various types of miso made from other beans, such as adzuki or chickpeas, which are not as common in Japan. Awase miso is a mixed miso that is usually mild in taste.

04.

05.

06.

IZAKAYA/BAR
FOOD

KAKIAGE
(JAPANESE FRITTERS)
かき揚げ

MAKES: 6 PREPARATION: 20 MINUTES COOKING: 15 MINUTES

FRESH

½ onion, thinly sliced

100 g (3½ oz) carrot, cut into thin
  matchsticks

100 g (3½ oz) small prawns (shrimp),
  peeled

10 g (¼ oz) flat-leaf parsley, roughly
  chopped

400 ml (14 fl oz) ice-cold sparkling
  water

PANTRY

3 cups (750 ml) sunflower oil,
  for deep-frying

120 g (4¼ oz) plus 2 tablespoons
  self-raising flour

100 g (3½ oz) tin corn kernels, drained

a pinch of sea salt and ground
  black pepper

These Japanese fritters are similar to an Indian bhaji.
One great thing about *kakiage* is that there are no strict
rules about the ingredients or possible combinations.
Try using other vegetables (root vegetables always
work well) and other types of seafood.

—

Heat the oil for deep-frying in a large, deep pan to 180°C (350°F).

Combine the 2 tablespoons flour with the vegetables, prawns and
parsley and lightly mix in a bowl.

Pour the sparkling water into a large bowl, sift the remaining flour
and the salt into the bowl and combine very gently with a whisk.
You don't need to mix it perfectly, and don't worry if the flour isn't
completely mixed in.

Add the flour-coated ingredients to the bowl and mix lightly.

Scoop up a ladle of the vegetable mixture and carefully drop it
into the hot oil. Use a spoon to keep the fritters together against the
side of the pan.

Cook the fritters for 30 seconds on one side, then flip and cook for
another minute. Lift the cooked fritters from the oil with a slotted
spoon. Shake to remove the excess oil, then place them on paper
towel to drain. Repeat with the rest of the mixture.

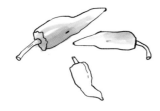

GANMODOKI
(DEEP-FRIED TOFU CAKE)
がんもどき

MAKES: 10 *PREPARATION: 15 MINUTES, PLUS 2-8 HOURS STANDING* *COOKING: 15 MINUTES*

FRESH

680 g (1 lb 8 oz) firm tofu

2 eggs, lightly beaten

40 g (1½ oz) carrots, cut into thin
  matchsticks

40 g (1½ oz) snow peas (mangetout),
  thinly sliced

freshly grated ginger, to serve

PANTRY

20 g (¾ oz) dried shiitake mushrooms,
  or 40 g (1½ oz) fresh shiitake, stalks
  removed and thinly sliced

1 tablespoon sake

a large pinch of sea salt

3 cups (750 ml) sunflower oil, for
  deep-frying

soy sauce, to serve

In Japan, we have specialised tofu shops where you can buy
fresh tofu in water, which is similar to buying freshly made
mozzarella from a proper Italian deli.

—

Place the tofu on a baking tray and top with another tray with
a 1 kg (2 lb 4 oz) weight on top. Leave it for 2 hours, or even
overnight, to press out the excess water.

If you are using dried shiitake mushrooms, soak them in a
bowl of hot water for 1 hour, then drain. Thinly slice the soaked
or fresh mushrooms, discarding the stalks.

Place the tofu in a food processor with the sake, eggs and salt
and blend until very smooth.

Tip the tofu mixture into a bowl and add the mushrooms, carrot
and snow peas. Combine well and then shape the mixture into
10 rounded patties.

Heat the oil in a deep frying pan over medium heat. When it
reaches 180°C (350°F), carefully slide the patties into the oil.
Cook two or three patties at a time for 3 minutes, turning
halfway through, until golden brown.

Remove the patties from the oil with a slotted spoon and place
them on paper towel to drain. Serve with a dash of soy sauce and
some grated ginger.

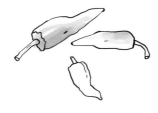

JAPANESE-STYLE POTATO SALAD

ポテトサラダ

*SERVES: 6 **PREPARATION**: 30 MINUTES **COOKING**: 30-40 MINUTES*

FRESH

500 g (1 lb 2 oz) fluffy potatoes
  (non-waxy potato, such as
  King Edward)

¼ large cucumber

2 eggs

¼ onion, thinly sliced

50 g (1¾ oz) ham, thinly sliced

PANTRY

½ tablespoon rice vinegar

a pinch of sea salt and
  ground black pepper

⅓ cup (85 g) mayonnaise
  (ideally Kewpie mayonnaise)

You might find it odd to have a potato salad recipe in a Japanese cookbook, but this is a popular dish, and if you go to Japan, you will encounter potato salad as a side dish on many occasions.

—

Place the whole potatoes in a steamer basket set over a saucepan of boiling water. Steam for 20–30 minutes, depending on the size of the potatoes. Check the water from time to time to make sure it doesn't dry out during cooking. Set the potatoes aside to cool a little, then peel them when they are cool enough to handle.

Coarsely mash the potatoes while they are still warm. Pour in the rice vinegar and mix well. Set aside to cool completely.

While the potatoes are cooling, prepare the rest of the ingredients. Cut the cucumber in half lengthways. Scrape out the seeds with a teaspoon, then slice thinly. Mix the salt through the cucumber. Leave to stand for 10 minutes, then squeeze out any excess water.

Bring a small saucepan of water to the boil over medium heat. Gently drop the eggs into the water and cook for 9–10 minutes. Cool the eggs under cold running water, then peel and finely chop them.

Add the cucumber, onion, egg, ham and mayonnaise to the mashed potatoes and mix well. Season with salt and pepper.

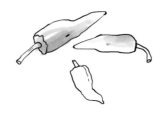

LOTUS ROOT CRISPS

レンコンチップス

SERVES: 4 PREPARATION: 10 MINUTES COOKING: 10 MINUTES

FRESH

220 g (7¾ oz) lotus root, peeled

PANTRY

300 ml (10½ fl oz) sunflower oil,
  for deep-frying

½ teaspoon sea salt, a pinch of aonori
  powder or shichimi togarashi
  (store-bought or homemade,
  see page 166), to serve

Lotus root has a long, woody body with a speckled beige skin. It can be found in the fresh or frozen section of Asian supermarkets. These crisps are not only great for snacking, but also make a fantastic garnish for salad or carpaccio.

—

Set a mandolin over a small bowl filled with cold water and cut the lotus root into paper-thin slices, about 1–2 mm (¹⁄₁₆ inch).

Heat the oil in a deep saucepan over medium–high heat until it reaches 180°C (350°F). Just before deep-frying, drain the lotus root and carefully pat it dry with paper towel.

Deep-fry the sliced lotus root in small batches, moving the slices around with a slotted spoon to keep them separated. Fry for 2 minutes, until golden. Lift out the crisps with a large slotted spoon and drain them on paper towel. Sprinkle with the sea salt, aonori powder or shichimi togarashi.

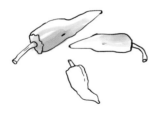

GRILLED SHIITAKE MUSHROOMS WITH GARLIC BUTTER

しいたけの醤油ガーリックバター焼き

SERVES: 4 PREPARATION: 10 MINUTES COOKING: 5-7 MINUTES

FRESH

16 large shiitake mushrooms,
    stalks removed

60 g (2¼ oz) butter, softened

4 garlic cloves, thinly sliced

½ lemon

PANTRY

3 tablespoons soy sauce

This is my favourite dish – it's super fast and easy to make, with an amazing flavour. It might sound odd, but the Japanese love the combined flavour of butter and soy sauce – it's very more-ish.

—

Preheat the grill to medium–high.

Make a cross-shaped incision in the centre of the gills of each mushroom – this will help them absorb the butter and soy sauce.

Place the mushrooms on a shallow baking tray, gill side up. Smear the butter on the gills and stems, then put 2–3 slices of garlic on top of each mushroom.

Set the tray under the hot grill and cook for 5–7 minutes, until the butter has melted, the garlic has turned golden brown and the mushrooms have softened slightly.

Transfer the mushrooms to a plate, drizzle with the soy sauce and squeeze the lemon over them before serving.

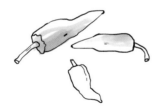

ROLLED OMELETTE

卵焼き

SERVES: 2-3 AS A SIDE DISH **PREPARATION:** *3 MINUTES* **COOKING:** *10 MINUTES*

FRESH

4 eggs

PANTRY

2 teaspoons light brown sugar

2 teaspoons soy sauce

1 teaspoon mirin

a pinch of sea salt

1 tablespoon sunflower oil, for oiling

This is a firm favourite in Japan and a classic staple in a bento box. The technique sounds challenging but, once you've mastered it, it's a fun and satisfying dish to cook.

—

01. Mix the eggs, sugar, soy sauce, mirin and salt in a measuring jug.

02. Wipe your egg roll pan (*tamagoyaki-ki*) or a 20 cm (8 inch) non-stick frying pan with oiled paper towel and heat over medium heat.

03. Pour one-quarter of the egg mixture into the pan. Tilt the pan to coat the bottom evenly and cook until the egg starts to set.

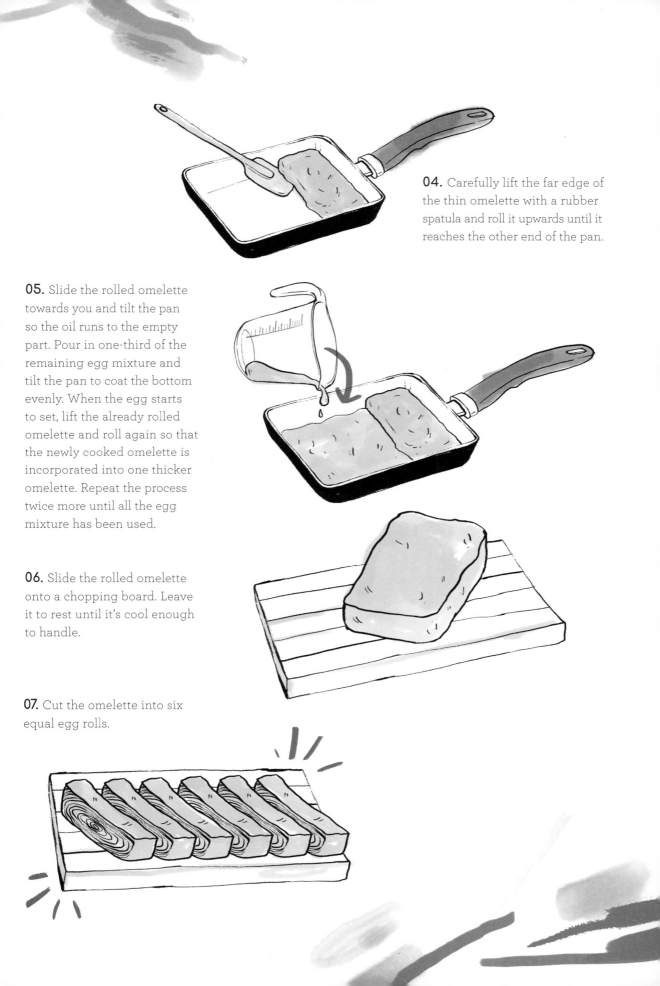

04. Carefully lift the far edge of the thin omelette with a rubber spatula and roll it upwards until it reaches the other end of the pan.

05. Slide the rolled omelette towards you and tilt the pan so the oil runs to the empty part. Pour in one-third of the remaining egg mixture and tilt the pan to coat the bottom evenly. When the egg starts to set, lift the already rolled omelette and roll again so that the newly cooked omelette is incorporated into one thicker omelette. Repeat the process twice more until all the egg mixture has been used.

06. Slide the rolled omelette onto a chopping board. Leave it to rest until it's cool enough to handle.

07. Cut the omelette into six equal egg rolls.

HOMEMADE ATSUAGE (FRIED TOFU)

手作り厚揚げ

SERVES: 2-4 *PREPARATION: 20 MINUTES* *COOKING: 15 MINUTES*

FRESH

640 g (1 lb 6 oz) firm tofu
(also called momen tofu),
cut into 8 large cubes

200 g (7 oz) cherry tomatoes,
quartered

2.5 cm (1 inch) piece of fresh
ginger, finely grated

PANTRY

3 cups (750 ml) sunflower oil,
for deep-frying

2 tablespoons extra virgin olive oil

2 teaspoons soy sauce

2 large pinches of sea salt

Although you can buy *atsuage* (chunky fried tofu) in some supermarkets and health-food stores, I have found that the *atsuage* from Asian grocery stores is of better quality.

—

Wrap the tofu in a clean, thick, cotton tea towel and place it on a baking tray for some of the excess liquid to drain away.

Heat the sunflower oil in a deep saucepan over medium–high heat until it reaches 180°C (350°F).

While the oil is heating, prepare the sauce. Mix the tomatoes, ginger, olive oil, soy sauce and salt together in a small bowl.

Deep-fry two to three tofu cubes at a time for 3 minutes until golden brown. Turn every few minutes to get an even golden colour on each side. Using a slotted spoon, carefully lift out the tofu and drain on paper towel.

Serve the tofu hot with the tomato and ginger sauce (grated daikon radish and soy sauce also works very well).

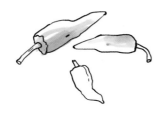

NASU DENGAKU (MISO EGGPLANT)

なす田楽

SERVES: 4 PREPARATION: 10 MINUTES COOKING: 20 MINUTES

FRESH

2 large eggplant (aubergines),
   halved lengthways and scored
   in a crisscross pattern

PANTRY

100 ml (3½ fl oz) sunflower oil

½ cup (125 ml) red miso

2 tablespoons light brown sugar

2 tablespoons mirin

1½ tablespoons sesame seeds

This is a well-loved, classic dish of melt-in-the-mouth, perfectly cooked eggplant with sweet and salty miso sauce. Try the miso sauce with Homemade Sesame Tofu (see page 70).

—

Slice 5 mm (¼ inch) off the skin side of the eggplant halves so that they will sit flat in the pan.

Heat half the oil in a large frying pan over medium heat. Place two of the eggplant halves in the pan, flesh side down. Cook for 3–4 minutes, until golden brown, then flip over. Cover with a lid and cook for a further 4 minutes, until the eggplant is soft and cooked through.

Remove the eggplant from the pan and wipe away any excess oil with paper towel. Repeat with the remaining oil and eggplant halves.

Preheat the grill to medium–high.

Place the eggplant in a shallow baking tray. Mix the miso, brown sugar and mirin in a small bowl. Spread the miso mixture over the cut side of the eggplant and grill for 2–3 minutes until the miso sauce is warmed through. Sprinkle with sesame seeds and serve.

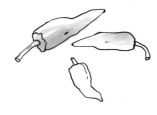

GRILLED PADRÓN PEPPERS WITH BONITO FLAKES

焼き唐辛子と鰹節

SERVES: 4 PREPARATION: 2 MINUTES COOKING: 5 MINUTES

FRESH

200 g (7 oz) peppers of your choice
(about 20 Padrón peppers or
4 Turkish long green peppers)

PANTRY

2 teaspoons sunflower oil

5 g (⅛ oz) katsuobushi (dried
bonito flakes)

2 tablespoons soy sauce

Fried Padrón peppers are a firm favourite at tapas bars. With simple ingredients, they're delicious and easy to prepare, just like this Japanese version.

—

Preheat the grill to the highest setting (about 250°C/500°F).

Place the whole peppers on a shallow baking tray and drizzle them with the oil.

Set the tray under the hot grill for 5 minutes, until the skin of the peppers blisters, scorches and begins to soften.

Just before serving, sprinkle the peppers with the katsuobushi and drizzle with the soy sauce.

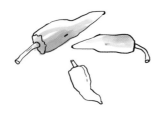

KARAAGE
(JAPANESE FRIED CHICKEN)

唐揚げ

SERVES: 4 *PREPARATION: 15 MINUTES, PLUS 30 MINUTES MARINATING* *COOKING: 15 MINUTES*

FRESH

1 egg white

2 garlic cloves, grated

3 cm (1¼ inch) piece of fresh ginger
(about 50 g/1¾ oz), peeled
and grated

600 g (1 lb 5 oz) boneless chicken
thighs with skin on, cut into
4–5 cm (1½–2 inch) pieces

PANTRY

2 tablespoons soy sauce

2 tablespoons sake

1 teaspoon toasted sesame oil

3 cups (750 ml) sunflower oil,
for deep-frying

100 g (3½ oz) cornflour (cornstarch)

Who doesn't love fried chicken? This garlicky and gingery Japanese version is tasty as it is, but also great served with grated daikon radish, Japanese-style potato salad (page 28) and ponzu dipping sauce (page 216).

—

Mix the soy sauce, sake, sesame oil, egg white, garlic and ginger together. Pour the mixture over the chicken in a bowl and mix well. Place in the fridge to marinate for 30 minutes.

Heat the sunflower oil in a deep saucepan over medium–high heat until it reaches 180°C (350°F).

Place the cornflour in a shallow dish, drop in the marinated chicken and toss to coat.

Slide one-third of the chicken pieces into the oil and cook for a few minutes until they just turn golden brown. Remove from the oil and leave to drain on paper towel while you cook the rest of the chicken.

Heat the sunflower oil to 190°C (375°F) and fry the chicken for a second time for 1–2 minutes, until golden all over.

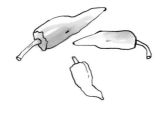

TUNA TATAKI

ツナのたたき

SERVES: 4 PREPARATION: 30 MINUTES COOKING: 15 MINUTES

FRESH

4 spring onions (scallions),
   thinly sliced lengthways

30 g (1 oz) fresh ginger, peeled
   and cut into thin matchsticks

200 g (7 oz) daikon radish,
   cut into thin matchsticks

3 garlic cloves, thinly sliced

400 g (14 oz) fresh tuna fillet
   (ideally a thin, long piece from
   the loin – ask your fishmonger
   or a Japanese grocery store)

4 shiso (perilla) leaves, thinly sliced
   (or baby cress, bottoms removed
   and leaves separated)

PANTRY

¼ cup (60 ml) sunflower oil

¼ teaspoon sea salt

3 tablespoons ponzu (store-bought
   or homemade, see page 216)

This is a simple yet indulgent dish, packed with flavour and texture. Meaty tuna, crispy garlic, ginger and aromatic shiso are an irresistible combination, ideal to serve with drinks.

—

Place the spring onion, ginger and daikon radish in a bowl of ice-cold water. This will help to keep them crisp.

Heat the sunflower oil in a small frying pan over medium heat. Fry the garlic until golden brown. Use a slotted spoon to transfer the garlic to a bowl and remove most of the excess oil from the pan with paper towel, leaving a little behind for the tuna.

Heat the pan over medium–high heat. Sprinkle salt all over the tuna and sear the tuna in the hot pan for 1 minute on each side. Remove the tuna from the pan and leave it to rest for 10 minutes, or until you are ready to serve. You can do this step in advance.

While resting the tuna, drain the water from the spring onion, daikon and ginger and pat dry with paper towel. Mix with the shiso leaves in a bowl.

Slice the tuna into 8 mm (⅜ inch) thick pieces (see page 124 to learn how to make sashimi).

Place the mixed salad on a plate and top with the sliced tuna, then scatter with the crispy garlic and drizzle with the ponzu.

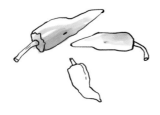

OKONOMIYAKI (JAPANESE SAVOURY PANCAKES)

お好み焼き

SERVES: 4 PREPARATION: 20 MINUTES COOKING: 30 MINUTES

FRESH

320 ml (11 fl oz) Basic Dashi Stock (see page 204 or use powdered dashi) or bonito dashi

4 eggs

400 g (14 oz) pointy green or white cabbage (about ¼ medium cabbage), finely shredded and chopped

160 g (5½ oz) king prawns (shrimp), peeled and deveined

360 ml (12 fl oz) tonkatsu sauce (store-bought or homemade, see page 214, but omit the sesame seeds and mustard) or okonomiyaki sauce (see page 18)

PANTRY

240 g (8½ oz) plain (all-purpose) flour

2 teaspoons baking powder

¼ cup (60 ml) sunflower oil

½ cup (120 g) mayonnaise (ideally Kewpie mayonnaise)

15 g (½ oz) katsuobushi (dried bonito flakes)

5 g (⅛ oz) aonori powder

Okonomi means 'as you like' in Japanese. As the name implies, you can mix in your favourite toppings... as you like! Think thinly sliced pork belly, beef, squid or even cheese (melty Cheddar cheese is great in these) and kimchi.

—

Mix the flour and baking powder in a bowl.

Whisk the dashi stock and eggs together in a jug. Pour into the flour and whisk it quickly, being careful not to overwork it. Add the cabbage and prawns and mix well.

Heat 1 teaspoon of the oil in a frying pan over medium heat and pour a small ladleful of the batter into the pan. Cook for 4 minutes until golden in colour and the edges have started to set. Flip over and cook for a further 4 minutes. Keep the okonomiyaki warm while you cook the remaining batter.

Pour the sauce over the okonomiyaki, then draw a zigzag shape over the top with the mayonnaise. Sprinkle with the katsuobushi and aonori powder.

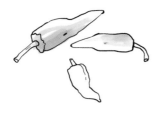

YAKITORI
(GRILLED CHICKEN SKEWERS)

焼き鳥

SERVES: 4 PREPARATION: 30 MINUTES COOKING: 10 MINUTES

FRESH

800 g (1 lb 12 oz) skinless chicken
   thigh fillets, excess fat trimmed
   and cut into 4 cm (1½ inch) cubes

8 spring onions (scallions),
   white part only, cut into 4 cm
   (1½ inch) pieces

½ cup (125 ml) teriyaki sauce
   (store-bought or homemade,
   see page 218)

PANTRY

12 bamboo skewers

4 teaspoons sunflower oil

½ teaspoon shichimi togarashi,
   (store-bought or homemade,
   see page 166)

There are numerous varieties of yakitori, including chicken offal
and skin, but the classic and probably most popular is *negima* –
chicken thigh and spring onion with a sweet soy sauce.

—

Soak the bamboo skewers in water for 15 minutes, as this will
prevent them from burning during grilling.

Spear the chicken and spring onions onto the soaked skewers –
there are no strict rules, but aim for a good mix of both chicken
and spring onion.

Heat the oil in a cast-iron frying pan over medium heat. When it
starts to sizzle, place the chicken skewers in the pan, cover with the
lid and cook for 4 minutes on each side or until cooked through.

Pour the teriyaki sauce into the pan, turn the skewers with tongs
and toss them with the sauce. As the sauce thickens, take the pan
off the heat.

Arrange the skewers on a serving plate, drizzle with the cooking
sauce, sprinkle with the shichimi togarashi and serve.

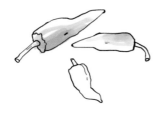

OCHAZUKE
(SALMON WITH TEA BROTH)

お茶漬け

SERVES: 4 **PREPARATION:** *10 MINUTES, PLUS 5-8 HOURS MARINATING* **COOKING:** *10 MINUTES*

FRESH

250 g (9 oz) salmon fillet

½ cup (40 g) good-quality Japanese
green tea leaves or 720 ml (25 fl oz)
Basic Dashi Stock (see page 204 or
use powdered dashi)

600 g (1 lb 5 oz) cooked Japanese rice
(see page 208)

30 g (1 oz) fresh ginger, peeled and
cut into thin matchsticks

PANTRY

½ tablespoon sake

2 teaspoons sea salt flakes

1 nori sheet

1½ tablespoons white sesame seeds,
toasted and roughly ground

2 teaspoons wasabi

This salt-cured salmon is not only great for this dish, but is also amazing as a main meal with Onigiri (Rice Balls) – see page 114. The salmon can be prepared in advance and chilled until needed.

—

Drizzle the sake over the salmon and spread it to cover each side. Sprinkle the salt over each side of the salmon and massage it into the flesh. Refrigerate the salmon for 5 hours (or ideally overnight).

Preheat the grill to medium–high.

Pat the salmon dry with paper towel and grill for 5 minutes on each side.

Toast the nori sheet by fanning it over the hob over very low heat. Be careful that it does not catch fire! Crumble the toasted nori and set aside.

Tip the tea leaves into a teapot and fill the teapot with boiling water. Brew for 2 minutes – the tea needs to be extra strong for this recipe.

Divide the rice among four bowls. Arrange the flaked salmon, ginger, sesame seeds, nori and wasabi on the rice. Pour the tea (or hot dashi) over the top and serve immediately.

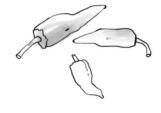

TOFU

01. TERIYAKI TOFU STEAK
照り焼き豆腐ステーキ

—

Cut 300 g (10½ oz) tofu (I prefer silken tofu) into 4 equal pieces and place on a double layer of paper towel. Drain for 10 minutes, then replace the paper towel and flip the tofu.

Spread 2 tablespoons cornflour (cornstarch) on a tray and dust the tofu all over.

Heat 2 teaspoons oil in a frying pan over medium heat. Add the tofu and cook on both sides for 2–3 minutes.

Spoon 3 tablespoons teriyaki sauce (store-bought or homemade, page 218) on top of the tofu, turn and cook for 1 minute. Serves 2.

02. MISO-MARINATED TOFU
豆腐の味噌漬け

—

Mix 200 g (7 oz) white miso (or any mixture of different kinds of miso) and 2 tablespoons mirin.

Spread half the miso mixture in a small container. Lay a piece of muslin large enough to wrap around the tofu on top of the miso mixture.

Cut 200 g (7 oz) firm tofu into 4 pieces and arrange it on the muslin. Fold the muslin over the tofu and cover the tofu with the rest of the miso mixture.

Keep the tofu refrigerated and eat it within a week. You can eat this the next day, but it's best after the third day. You can reuse the miso mixture a couple of times for this purpose. Serves 4–8.

03. QUICK TOFU CHEESECAKE
豆腐チーズケーキ

—

Break up 100 g (3½ oz) silken tofu in a bowl. Add ¾ cup (200 g) Greek yoghurt, 100 g (3½ oz) cream cheese, the grated zest of ½ organic, unwaxed lemon and 2 teaspoons caster (superfine) sugar. Blend until very smooth.

Pour the tofu mixture into a very fine sieve and drain for 15 minutes.

Crush 4 digestive biscuits finely and divide them among four small glasses.

Spoon the tofu mixture over the biscuits and chill for 30–45 minutes.

Macerate 6 strawberries that have been cut into small cubes in 1 teaspoon caster sugar.

Spoon the macerated strawberries over the cheesecake to serve. Serves 4.

04. TOFU & CUCUMBER COLD POTAGE SHOT
冷製豆腐ポタージュスープ

—

Combine 150 g (5½ oz) silken tofu, 150 ml (5 fl oz) Basic Dashi Stock (see page 204 or use powdered dashi), 100 ml (3½ fl oz) soy milk, 1½ teaspoons soy sauce and a large pinch of sea salt in a blender or food processor and blend until smooth. Chill for 30–45 minutes.

Serve in small glasses. Top with 120 g (4¼ oz) cucumber that has been diced into 3 mm (⅛ inch) pieces and 20 g (¾ oz) finely chopped Pickled Ginger (see page 180). Serves 4.

05. CRISPY TOFU CROUTONS
豆腐クルトン

—

Cut 200 g (7 oz) firm tofu into 1.5 cm (⅝ inch) cubes. Drain on paper towel for 10 minutes to get rid of any excess liquid. Flip the tofu and replace the paper towel.

Heat 150 ml (5 fl oz) sunflower oil in a saucepan over medium heat. When the oil reaches 180°C (350°F), fry the tofu for 2 minutes. Scoop out the crispy tofu using a slotted spoon. Drain on paper towel.

Sprinkle the tofu with sea salt. Serve it as a snack or serve with a salad as croutons. Serves 4.

06. TOFU DIP
豆腐ディップ

—

Place 10 g (¼ oz) white sesame seeds in a small frying pan over low heat. Toast them gently. Shake the pan from time to time to prevent burning. As soon as you hear the sesame seeds popping, take the pan off the heat and leave them to cool down.

Transfer the seeds to a *suribachi* or mortar and coarsely grind them.

Break 200 g (7 oz) firm tofu into pieces and put it in a blender or food processor with 1 tablespoon soy sauce, 1 teaspoon light brown sugar, 4 teaspoons mirin and 2 teaspoons white miso. Blend until smooth.

Mix in the ground sesame seeds. This tastes great with crudités or grilled vegetables. Makes about 200 g (7 oz).

GYOZA DUMPLINGS

餃子

MAKES: 52 PREPARATION: 45 MINUTES COOKING: 7 MINUTES PER BATCH

FRESH

300 g (10½ oz) Chinese cabbage (wong bok), finely chopped

300 g (10½ oz) pork mince

3 spring onions (scallions), finely chopped

20 g (¾ oz) fresh ginger, peeled and finely grated

3 garlic cloves, finely chopped

PANTRY

½ teaspoon sea salt

1½ tablespoons soy sauce

1 tablespoon toasted sesame oil

1 tablespoon sake

52 gyoza wrappers (thawed if frozen)

2 teaspoons plain (all-purpose) flour, plus extra for dusting

sunflower oil, for frying

Tip: The round, white gyoza wrappers can be found in the fresh or frozen section of good Asian grocery stores.

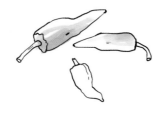

This is a fun dish to make with a bunch of people. Get your family and friends involved to create a production line and make a big batch of dumplings.

—

Sprinkle the salt over the cabbage, mix and leave for 10 minutes.

Mix the pork, spring onion, ginger, garlic, soy sauce, sesame oil and sake in a bowl. Squeeze any excess liquid from the cabbage. Add the cabbage to the pork mixture and combine well.

Lay as many gyoza wrappers as you have room for on a clean work surface and have a small bowl of water to hand.

Spoon ½ tablespoon of the filling onto each wrapper. Wet the top half of the wrapper, fold it over the filling to seal and make three to five pleats. Lay the dumplings on a tray that has been dusted with a little flour to prevent them from sticking.

Pour 1 teaspoon oil into a frying pan and arrange 13 dumplings, upright, in the pan. Heat over medium–high heat and cook for about 2 minutes until you hear sizzling sounds.

Mix ¼ cup (60 ml) water with ½ teaspoon of the flour. Pour it into the pan, cover with the lid and cook for 2 minutes.

Remove the lid, increase the heat and cook until the liquid has evaporated and the base of the dumplings has become crisp. Turn off the heat and cover the pan with a plate. Carefully flip the pan upside down to transfer the dumplings to the plate. Repeat until all the ingredients have been used.

Serve the dumplings with some Crispy Garlic & Chilli Oil (see page 174), Ponzu (see page 216) or soy sauce and rice vinegar for dipping.

KINPIRA
(SOY CARROT & PARSNIP)

人参とパースニップのきんぴら

SERVES: 4 PREPARATION: 10 MINUTES COOKING: 5 MINUTES

FRESH

200 g (7 oz) carrots, cut into
long thin matchsticks

200 g (7 oz) parsnips, celeriac
or potatoes, cut into long
thin matchsticks

PANTRY

2 tablespoons white sesame seeds

1½ tablespoons toasted sesame oil

1 small dried chilli, thinly sliced

4 teaspoons soy sauce

4 teaspoons mirin

This is a simple and delicious side dish that can be made
in just a few minutes. Traditional recipes don't include
parsnip, but they really are delicious with the carrot, as
are potato and celeriac.

—

Gently toast the sesame seeds in a small frying pan over low
heat, shaking the pan from time to time to prevent burning.
As soon as you hear the sesame seeds popping, take the
pan off the heat and leave them to cool down.

Heat the sesame oil with the dried chilli in a frying pan over
medium heat. Add the carrot and parsnip and stir-fry for
2 minutes. Add the soy sauce and mirin and cook for 2–3 minutes,
until the liquid has been absorbed by the vegetables.

Sprinkle the sesame seeds on top to serve.

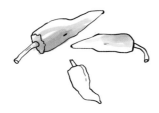

SIDE
DISHES

BRAISED DAIKON
WITH PORK MISO

ふろふき大根と肉味噌

SERVES: 4 PREPARATION: 10 MINUTES COOKING: 40 MINUTES

FRESH

800 g (1 lb 12 oz) daikon radish,
   cut into 4 cm (1½ inch) rings

250 g (9 oz) pork mince

grated zest of ½ organic, unwaxed
   lemon

PANTRY

8 cm (3¼ inch) square piece of kombu
   (dried kelp)

¼ cup (60 ml) red miso

2 teaspoons light brown sugar

2 tablespoons mirin

When turnips or kohlrabi are in season, consider using them instead of the daikon radish. For a vegetarian version, omit the pork, but mix together the miso, sugar and mirin to make a lovely sweet miso topping.

—

If you look at the cut side of the daikon from above, you can see a loop of fibre inside the peel. Use a knife to remove that part, along with the skin. Make a crisscross incision on one side of the daikon, which will help the daikon to cook faster.

Place the piece of kombu in the base of a saucepan and add the daikon, with the incision side down. Pour over enough water to just cover the daikon. Bring to the boil over medium heat. Reduce the heat to a simmer and cook for 30–40 minutes, until the daikon is soft enough for a skewer to pass through easily.

Meanwhile, prepare the pork. Heat a frying pan over medium heat and fry the pork for 5–8 minutes, until just cooked through.

Combine the miso, brown sugar and mirin in a small bowl, then pour into the pan. Mix well, turn off the heat and set aside.

Place the daikon in a small bowl with a little of the cooking liquid. Spoon the pork mixture on top of the daikon and garnish with the lemon zest.

GRILLED EGGPLANT
WITH GINGER

焼きなすと生姜

SERVES: 4 **PREPARATION:** *10 MINUTES* **COOKING:** *15-20 MINUTES*

FRESH

2 large eggplant (aubergines),
about 330 g (11½ oz) each

2 spring onions (scallions),
finely shredded

30 g (1 oz) fresh ginger, peeled
and grated

PANTRY

¼ cup (60 ml) soy sauce

This dish reminds me of Japanese summers, when eggplant
is in season. It's a great accompaniment to udon or soba
noodles with a cold broth.

—

Heat a chargrill pan over medium heat. Put the whole eggplant
in the pan and grill for about 15-20 minutes, turning often, until
the skin is charred. Test with a skewer to see if the eggplant are
soft enough. Don't worry much if the skin is really charred since
the smokiness is an important part of this dish's flavour.

When the eggplant are cool enough to handle, peel the skin from
the top to the bottom. Cut both eggplant in half lengthways, then
cut each half into two strips so that you have eight long pieces.

Serve the eggplant strips in a bowl, topped with the spring onion
and grated ginger, and drizzled with the soy sauce.

SUNOMONO (WAKAME, CUCUMBER & PRAWN)

わかめ、きゅうり、エビの酢の物

SERVES: 4   PREPARATION: 30 MINUTES   COOKING: 2 MINUTES

FRESH

½ cucumber, peeled and cut in half lengthways

6 large prawns (shrimp), peeled

2 tablespoons Basic Dashi Stock (see page 204 or use powdered dashi)

2.5 cm (1 inch) piece of fresh ginger, peeled and cut into thin matchsticks

PANTRY

a large pinch of sea salt

10 g (¼ oz) dried wakame

2 tablespoons rice vinegar

1 teaspoon soy sauce

1 teaspoon light brown sugar

This refreshing salad is a typical side dish for a Japanese table and it's a great palate cleanser. You can replace the prawns with octopus or white crab meat.

—

Remove the seeds from the cucumber using a teaspoon and slice it thinly. Add the salt and toss to coat. Leave the cucumber to stand for 5 minutes, then squeeze out any excess water.

Soak the wakame in a small bowl of water for about 5 minutes, then drain.

Bring a small saucepan of water to the boil over medium heat. Add the prawns and boil for 2 minutes. Drain and leave to cool. Once cooled, cut the prawns in half lengthways and remove the vein from the back.

Mix the dashi, vinegar, soy sauce and sugar in a small bowl until the sugar has dissolved.

Assemble the cucumber, wakame, prawns and ginger in a bowl and pour the dressing over the top to serve.

GREEN BEANS WITH SESAME DRESSING

いんげん豆の胡麻和え

SERVES: 4 **PREPARATION:** *15 MINUTES* **COOKING:** *5 MINUTES*

FRESH

400 g (14 oz) green beans, trimmed

PANTRY

¼ cup (40 g) white sesame seeds

3 tablespoons light brown sugar

3 tablespoons soy sauce

a pinch of sea salt

Tip: A *suribachi* bowl (mortar) and *surikogi* stick (pestle) are very useful to have in the kitchen. They are widely available in Japanese grocery stores or online.

Sesame seeds are one of Japan's most fundamental ingredients. Toasted sesame seeds are widely available, but I recommend lightly re-toasting them to boost the aroma and flavour – it will make a significant difference to the dish.

—

Gently toast the sesame seeds in a small frying pan over low heat, shaking the pan from time to time to prevent burning. As soon as you hear the sesame seeds popping, take the pan off the heat and leave them to cool down.

Transfer the sesame seeds to a *suribachi* or mortar and coarsely grind them. Add the brown sugar and soy sauce and mix until the sugar has dissolved.

Bring a saucepan of water to the boil over high heat. Add the salt and blanch the beans for 3 minutes.

Drain the beans, rinse them under cold running water and, when completely cooled, pat dry with paper towel.

Just before serving, mix the beans with the sesame dressing.

TOFU, TOMATO & SHISO SALAD

豆腐,トマトと紫蘇のサラダ

SERVES: 4 *PREPARATION: 15 MINUTES* *COOKING: 5 MINUTES*

FRESH

600 g (1 lb 5 oz) silken tofu, drained and cut into 1 cm (½ inch) slices

10 cherry tomatoes, halved

15 g (½ oz) shiso (perilla) leaves, thinly sliced, or coriander (cilantro) leaves

3 cm (1¼ inch) piece of fresh ginger, peeled, cut into thin matchsticks and kept in cold water

3 tablespoons Japanese Onion Dressing (see page 162)

PANTRY

20 g (¾ oz) almonds

This is an interesting combination of tomato, tofu, nuts and aromatic herbs. If you don't have the onion dressing, simply serve the tofu with soy sauce and extra virgin olive oil or Crispy Garlic and Chilli Oil (see page 174).

—

Preheat the oven to 170°C (325°F) and toast the almonds until they release their nutty smell. Remove from the oven and leave to cool. When the almonds are cool enough to handle, roughly chop them.

Put the tofu on a serving platter and scatter the almonds, tomatoes, herbs and drained ginger over the top. Pour the dressing over the salad to serve.

HOMEMADE SESAME TOFU

胡麻豆腐

SERVES: 8 **PREPARATION:** *10 MINUTES, PLUS 3-8 HOURS SETTING* **COOKING:** *10 MINUTES*

FRESH

400 ml (14 fl oz) filtered water,
  mineral water or Kombu Dashi
  Stock (see page 206)

PANTRY

80 g (2¾ oz) arrowroot

a pinch of sea salt

60 g (2¼ oz) tahini

soy sauce and wasabi or sweet miso
  (Nasu Dengaku, see page 38),
  to serve

This rich sesame tofu is enjoyable simply with soy sauce and
wasabi, but is also great with sweet miso. Use the sweet miso
recipe included in the recipe for Nasu Dengaku (see page 38).

—

Line a 900 g (2 lb) loaf tin with plastic wrap.

Mix the arrowroot, water (or dashi) and salt in a small bowl.
Set a fine strainer over a saucepan and strain the mixture
to get rid of any lumps.

Add the tahini to the pan and cook over medium heat, stirring
constantly with a whisk (the mixture can burn very easily) for
about 8-10 minutes, until it has a thick white sauce consistency.

Pour the mixture into the prepared tin and spread evenly.
Transfer to the fridge to set for at least 3 hours, or overnight.

Cut the firmed sesame tofu into eight pieces and serve with
soy sauce and wasabi or a sweet miso.

LEAF SALAD WITH UMEBOSHI DRESSING

チコリのサラダと梅ドレッシング

SERVES: 4 PREPARATION: 10 MINUTES

FRESH

4 large red and white witlof (endive)

2 tablespoons chervil or chives

PANTRY

2 tablespoons umeboshi paste

2 tablespoons rice vinegar

2 tablespoons sunflower oil

2 teaspoons light brown sugar

4 g (⅛ oz) katsuobushi
(dried bonito flakes)

The bitter leaves and sweet-and-sour dressing are a perfect palate cleanser. Umeboshi are pickled *ume* fruit, which are similar to plums or apricots. They are extremely salty and sour, so they're often used as a condiment or sauce.

—

Mix the umeboshi paste, vinegar, oil, sugar, katsuobushi and 2 tablespoons water together.

Cut the bottom off the witlof and separate the leaves. Wash the leaves and drain in a colander.

Mix the dressing and leaves just before serving. Arrange on a plate and sprinkle with the chervil.

SHIRAAE
(TOFU & SESAME PASTE)

白和え

SERVES: 4 *PREPARATION: 20 MINUTES, PLUS 30 MINUTES DRAINING* *COOKING: 5 MINUTES*

FRESH

340 g (11¾ oz) firm tofu

8 fresh shiitake mushrooms, stalks removed, sliced

½ carrot, peeled and cut into matchsticks

100 g (3½ oz) English spinach, thick stalks removed and cut into 3 cm (1¼ inch) pieces

PANTRY

2 pinches of sea salt

2 tablespoons soy sauce

1 teaspoon light brown sugar

2 tablespoons mirin

2 teaspoons miso

15 g (½ oz) white sesame seeds

This dish reminds me of good-quality hummus. Actually, this tofu paste is amazing as a dipping sauce for vegetable sticks, when you add a little more seasoning (see page 52 for a delicious tofu dip).

—

Wrap the tofu in paper towel and place it on a plate. Place a similar-sized plate on top and add a 500 g (1 lb 2 oz) weight. Transfer to the fridge for 30 minutes for the liquid to drain.

Meanwhile, prepare the vegetables. Place a frying pan over medium heat and fry the shiitake mushrooms for 2 minutes, then remove and set aside.

Add the carrot, 50 ml (1½ fl oz) water and a pinch of salt to the same pan. Steam for 2 minutes. Tip the carrots into a colander to drain. Repeat the same process with the spinach. Tip the spinach into the colander with the carrots and run them under cold water to cool. Squeeze the vegetables with your hands to remove the liquid.

Break the drained tofu into pieces. Combine the tofu with the soy sauce, sugar, mirin and miso and blend until smooth.

Grind the sesame seeds in a mortar and pestle or spice grinder. Just before serving, mix the tofu purée, vegetables and ground sesame seeds together. Mix well.

EGG

01. HOT SPRING POACHED EGGS
温泉卵

—

Bring 4 cups (1 litre) water to the boil and take it off heat. Add 200 ml (7 fl oz) room temperature water to the pan. Add 2 eggs to the water and leave to stand for 14 minutes.

Remove the eggs from the water and leave to stand for 3 minutes.

Crack the eggs and serve. Serves 2.

02. CHAWANMUSHI (SAVOURY EGG CUSTARD)
茶碗蒸し

—

Bring a saucepan of water to the boil over high heat. The depth of the water needs to be half the height of the heatproof cups you are using.

Mix 2 lightly beaten eggs, 400 ml (14 fl oz) chilled Basic Dashi Stock (see page 204), 2 teaspoons soy sauce and a large pinch of salt. Strain the egg mixture into a bowl.

Divide 8 peeled and deveined king prawns (shrimp), 2 thinly sliced shiitake mushrooms and 230 g (8 oz) wilted English spinach (excess water squeezed out) among four heatproof cups and pour in the egg mixture. Top with 8 matchstick strips of lemon zest. Cover each cup with foil and seal tightly.

Turn down the pan of boiling water to medium heat. Gently place the cups in the pan, cover with a lid and steam for 5 minutes. Turn off the heat and set aside for 15 minutes without removing the lid from the pan. Serve immediately. Serves 4.

03. JAPANESE EGG DROP SOUP
かきたま汁

—

Bring 800 ml (28 fl oz) Basic Dashi Stock (see page 204) to the boil in a saucepan over medium heat. Add 1 tablespoon soy sauce, 2 teaspoons sake, ¼ teaspoon sea salt and 10 g (¼ oz) peeled and finely grated fresh ginger.

Combine 3 tablespoons water with 3 tablespoons cornflour (cornstarch) in a bowl. Take the pan off the heat and mix in the cornflour mixture.

Place the pan back on the heat and cook until the soup thickens. Pour in 2 lightly beaten eggs, slowly swirling around the pan. When the egg is partially set, serve in bowls with a sprinkle of thinly sliced spring onions (scallions). Serves 4.

04. SOY-MARINATED BOILED EGGS
醤油卵

—

Mix 75 ml (2¼ fl oz) soy sauce, 150 ml (5 fl oz) sake and 3 tablespoons mirin in a saucepan and bring to the boil. Add 2 g (1/16 oz) katsuobushi and leave to cool.

Bring a small saucepan of water to the boil over high heat. Add 2 eggs and reduce the heat to medium. Cook the eggs for 8 minutes, then remove and cool under cold water.

Peel the cooled eggs and place them in the sauce. Refrigerate the eggs in the sauce for 1–3 days. Consume within 3 days. Serves 2.

05. KINSHI TAMAGO (EGG CREPES)
錦糸卵

—

Beat 2 eggs, ½ teaspoon caster (superfine) sugar, ½ teaspoon sake and a pinch of sea salt together in a bowl. Prepare a wet tea towel.

Heat a non-stick frying pan over medium-low heat. Wipe the pan with oiled paper towel. Pour one-third of the egg mixture into the pan and swirl to cover the base of the pan. Cook until the egg starts to set, then take the pan off the heat and cover with the wet tea towel for 1 minute.

Remove the tea towel. Place the pan back on the heat, cover with a lid and cook for another minute. Remove the crepe with a spatula and place on a chopping board. Repeat.

Stack 3 sheets of crepes and roll them together. Cut them into 3 mm (⅛ inch) thick slices. Makes 3 sheets.

06. MISO-MARINATED EGG YOLKS
黄身の味噌漬け

—

Mix 80 g (2¾ oz) white miso with 1 tablespoon mirin. Spread half of the miso mixture in a container and make two dents with the back of a rolling pin. Lay a muslin cloth over the miso and put 2 egg yolks in the dents. Lay another piece of muslin on top. Cover the yolks with the remaining miso.

Cover the container and keep in the fridge for 4 days. The yolks should be firm with a jelly-like texture and a vibrant orange colour. Makes 2.

AGEDASHI TOFU (FRIED TOFU & EGGPLANT)

揚げ出し豆腐

SERVES: 4 PREPARATION: 20 MINUTES COOKING: 30 MINUTES

FRESH

600 g (1 lb 5 oz) silken tofu

2 cups (500 ml) Basic Dashi Stock
(see page 204 or use powdered dashi)

1 eggplant (aubergine), about 270 g
(9½ oz), cut into 3 cm (1¼ inch)
wedges and scored in a crisscross
pattern

2 spring onions (scallions), cut into
thin matchsticks and kept in
cold water

PANTRY

2½ tablespoons soy sauce

1½ tablespoons light brown sugar
or mirin

30 g (1 oz) cornflour (cornstarch)
or plain (all-purpose) flour

350 ml (12 fl oz) sunflower oil

shichimi togarashi (store-bought or
homemade, see page 166), to serve

Tip: As an alternative to using the
dashi broth, soy sauce and sugar, you
could use 2 tablespoons Mentsuyu
(see page 212) mixed with 450 ml
(16 fl oz) warm water.

This is a surprisingly rich and satisfying dish that non-vegetarians will also enjoy. Serve with Smoked Mackerel & Ginger Japanese Pilaf (see page 112) and Green Beans with Sesame Dressing (see page 66).

—

Cut the tofu into eight equal pieces. Place on a double layer of paper towel and leave for 5 minutes, then replace the paper towel, turn the tofu over and leave for a further 5 minutes.

Heat a small saucepan over medium heat and warm the dashi, soy sauce and sugar (or use Mentsuyu and warm water, see Tip below). Set aside.

Place the cornflour in a shallow dish and dust the tofu on each side just before frying.

Warm the oil in a frying pan over medium heat to 160°C (320°F). Gently slide the tofu into the pan and fry until golden on each side. Carefully lift out the tofu with a slotted spoon and drain on paper towel. Fry the eggplant in the hot oil until golden on each side. Drain on paper towel to remove any excess oil.

Reheat the broth if needed. Divide the tofu and eggplant between four bowls and pour the warm broth on top. Sprinkle with spring onion and shichimi togarashi to serve.

ONION & FENNEL SALAD

玉ねぎとフェンネル、鰹節のサラダ

*SERVES: 4 **PREPARATION:** 15 MINUTES*

FRESH

1 white onion

½ fennel bulb, about 200 g (7 oz)

PANTRY

1 g (¹⁄₁₆ oz) katsuobushi (dried bonito flakes)

a pinch of shichimi togarashi (store-bought or homemade, see page 166), to serve

75 ml (2¼ fl oz) ponzu (store-bought or homemade, see page 216)

Normally, we only use onions for this recipe, but the subtle aniseed flavour of fennel works surprisingly well with this dish, so I decided to add it. Spanish or Italian white onions tend to be sweeter, so I recommend using those.

—

Fill a large bowl with ice-cold water. Set a mandolin over the bowl and slice the onion and fennel into paper-thin slices. Leave the vegetables in the water for 10 minutes, or until they crisp up. This process will also help to get rid of any harsh onion taste.

Drain the vegetables in a colander. Arrange the onion and fennel on plates, sprinkle with the katsuobushi and shichimi togarashi and drizzle the ponzu on top just before serving.

MISO SOUP WITH GRILLED EGGPLANT & SESAME

茄子と練りごまの味噌汁

SERVES: 4 PREPARATION: 5 MINUTES COOKING: 20 MINUTES

FRESH

170 g (5¾ oz) eggplant (aubergine),
    halved lengthways and cut into
    5 mm slices

3 cups (750 ml) Basic Dashi Stock
    (see page 204 or use powdered dashi)

⅔ cup (20 g) rocket (arugula)

PANTRY

4 teaspoons white sesame seeds

5 teaspoons tahini

¼ cup (60 ml) red miso

The eggplant and sesame flavour combination is quite common in Middle-Eastern cooking. Japanese traditional cooking also features this delicious combination.

—

Gently toast the sesame seeds in a small frying pan over low heat, shaking the pan from time to time to prevent burning. As soon as you hear the sesame seeds popping, take the pan off the heat and leave them to cool down.

Transfer the sesame seeds to a *suribachi* or mortar and coarsely grind them.

Heat a chargrill pan over high heat. Grill the eggplant for 2 minutes on each side. Remove from the pan and set aside.

Heat the dashi in a saucepan over medium heat until almost boiling, then reduce the heat to low.

Mix the tahini and miso in a small bowl, then add a ladle of dashi stock. Mix until the miso has dissolved, then pour the liquid back into the pan. Heat again until just below boiling point – do not allow the soup to boil.

Arrange the grilled eggplant in a bowl and pour the soup over the top. Serve topped with the sesame seeds and rocket.

SAKE-STEAMED CLAMS

あさりの酒蒸し

SERVES: 4 **PREPARATION:** *10 MINUTES, PLUS 1 HOUR STANDING* **COOKING:** *5-10 MINUTES*

FRESH

1 kg (2 lb 4 oz) clams

30 g (1 oz) fresh ginger, peeled and
cut into thin matchsticks

8 spring onions, cut into 5 cm (2 inch)
pieces and sliced into long
thin strips

PANTRY

30 g (1 oz) sea salt

150 ml (5 fl oz) sake

This is a wonderful dish that can be made with very little
effort if you are short on time. However, it's important to
prepare the clams properly to remove all grit and sand.

—

To remove the grit from the clams, mix 4 cups (1 litre) cold
water with the sea salt in a large bowl and stir until the salt
has dissolved.

Place the clams in a large deep tray and pour the salted water
over the clams until they are almost covered. Cover the tray with
a tea towel and leave it in a dark, cool place for 1 hour (or in the
fridge overnight).

Drain the clams in a colander and wash them in cold running
water. Check the clams – they should be tightly closed. Discard
any half-opened clams or any that don't close when tapped.

Combine the clams, ginger, spring onion and sake in a large
saucepan or wok and cover the pan with a lid. Cook the clams
over medium–high heat for 5–10 minutes. Remove the lid and
check the clams. If all of the clams are wide open, the dish is
ready. Discard any unopened shells.

MISO SOUP WITH PORK & WINTER ROOT VEGETABLES

豚汁

*SERVES: 4 **PREPARATION:** 10 MINUTES **COOKING:** 25 MINUTES*

FRESH

400 g (14 oz) pork shoulder steak,
cut into 5 mm (¼ inch) slices, or
thinly sliced pork belly, trimmed
of any excess fat

240 g (8½ oz) daikon radish,
sliced and quartered

200 g (7 oz) carrots, halved lengthways
and cut into 5 mm (¼ inch) slices

240 g (8½ oz) Jerusalem artichokes
(about 4 medium) or 1 burdock,
peeled and sliced into rings

6 spring onions (scallions),
thinly sliced on the diagonal

PANTRY

½ teaspoon sunflower oil

90 ml (3 fl oz) white miso

shichimi togarashi (store-bought or
homemade, see page 166), optional

This soup is a winter staple in Japan. Traditionally, it's made using a vegetable called burdock, which is not widely available outside Japan. Since I moved to London, I have discovered the Jerusalem artichoke, which is similar to the earthy flavour of burdock, and works perfectly in this soup.

—

Heat the oil in a saucepan over medium heat. Add the pork, then add the daikon, carrot and artichokes. Fry for 3 minutes.

Add 6 cups (1.5 litres) water and bring to the boil. Skim the fat off the surface as the soup cooks. Cook until the vegetables are softened, which should take about 15 minutes.

Put the miso in a small bowl and mix in a small amount of the cooking liquid. Stir well until the miso is completely dissolved. Pour this liquid back into the pan. Reduce the heat and gently cook for 5 minutes. Do not allow the soup to boil at this point.

Ladle the soup into bowls and top with the spring onion. Add a dash of shichimi togarashi if you want your soup to have a little spicy kick.

ONE BOWL

TERIYAKI CHICKEN ON RICE

照り焼きチキン丼

SERVES: 4 ***PREPARATION:*** *15 MINUTES* ***COOKING:*** *15 MINUTES*

FRESH

4 boneless chicken thighs with
  skin on, about 200 g (7 oz) each

90 ml (3 fl oz) teriyaki sauce
  (store-bought or homemade,
  see page 218)

1 quantity of Steamed Rice
  (see page 208)

4 spring onions (scallions),
  thinly sliced

PANTRY

2 nori sheets

a pinch of shichimi togarashi
  (store-bought or homemade,
  see page 166)

Everyone loves this dish, from kids to adults. Cook extra chicken as it is just as great in a lunchbox the next day.

—

Pierce the chicken skin with a fork; this will help the chicken to absorb the sauce and help to release any excess fat.

Heat a frying pan over medium–low heat. Place the chicken in the pan, skin side down (no oil is needed). The chicken will release some of its fat. Cook for about 9–10 minutes, until the chicken skin begins to crisp. Use paper towel to remove some of the fat if needed. Turn the chicken and cook for 4–6 minutes, until cooked through.

Pour the teriyaki sauce into the pan. Toss the chicken in the sauce and cook for 1 minute. Remove the pan from the heat and slice the cooked chicken into strips.

Divide the steamed rice among four bowls. Crush the nori in between your fingers and sprinkle it over the rice. Top the rice with the sliced chicken and spring onion. Finish the dish with a pinch of shichimi togarashi.

FRIED EGGPLANT WITH COLD UDON NOODLES

揚げなすと玉ねぎの薄切りをのせた冷やしうどん

SERVES: 4 *PREPARATION: 15 MINUTES* *COOKING: 15 MINUTES*

FRESH

450 ml (16 fl oz) Basic Dashi Stock
(see page 204 or use powdered
dashi)

½ onion, peeled and quartered

1 eggplant (aubergine), about
300 g (10½ oz)

300 g (10½ oz) daikon radish,
peeled and grated

PANTRY

2½ tablespoons soy sauce

1½ tablespoons light brown sugar

1 cup (250 ml) sunflower oil

1 kg (2 lb 4 oz) frozen udon noodles
or 400 g (14 oz) dried udon noodles

a pinch of shichimi togarashi
(store-bought or homemade,
see page 166), to serve

Tip: As an alternative to using the
dashi broth, soy sauce and sugar, you
could use ¼ cup (60 ml) Mentsuyu
(see page 212) mixed with 450 ml
(16 fl oz) water instead.

This is a perfect summer dish of refreshing cold udon noodles
in a chilled broth with tender fried eggplant. Try it with a hot
spring poached egg (see page 76).

—

Mix the dashi, soy sauce and sugar together (or use Mentsuyu
and water, see Tip below), then transfer to the fridge to chill.

Fill a bowl with ice-cold water. Set a mandolin over the bowl and
slice the onion very finely into the bowl. Leave the onion in the
water until serving time.

Cut the eggplant in half lengthways, then into 12 finger-sized
sticks. Heat the oil in a deep saucepan over medium heat. Fry the
eggplant for 3 minutes, until golden brown. Remove the eggplant
from the pan with a slotted spoon and drain on paper towel.

Cook the udon noodles according to the packet instructions,
then drain and rinse under cold running water until cool.

Divide the noodles among four deep bowls. Top the noodles with
the fried eggplant, onion and daikon. Pour the chilled broth over
the noodles and sprinkle with shichimi togarashi, if using.

KITSUNE UDON (UDON IN HOT BROTH WITH FRIED TOFU)

きつねうどん

SERVES: 4 PREPARATION: 10 MINUTES COOKING: 15 MINUTES

FRESH

4 aburaage (thin, fried tofu),
    cut diagonally into quarters

1.2 litres (42 fl oz) Basic Dashi
    (see page 204 or use powdered
    dashi)

4 spring onions (scallions),
    thinly sliced

PANTRY

3½ tablespoons soy sauce

5 tablespoons light brown sugar

2 teaspoons mirin

1 kg (2 lb 4 oz) frozen udon noodles
    or 400 g (14 oz) dried udon noodles

a pinch of shichimi togarashi
    (store-bought or homemade,
    see page 166), optional

Tip: As an alternative to using the
dashi broth, soy sauce and sugar, you
could use 90 ml (3 fl oz) Mentsuyu
(see page 212) mixed with 1.3 litres
(45 fl oz) warm water instead.

Aburaage is thin, fried tofu – similar to *atsuage* (see page 36), but thinner and fluffier. It is sold fresh or frozen in most Asian grocery stores.

—

Bring a small saucepan of water to the boil over high heat, then reduce the heat to low. Add the fried tofu and simmer for 2 minutes. Remove the pan from the heat and gently squeeze the tofu to get rid of any excess oil.

Combine 150 ml (5 fl oz) water with 2 tablespoons of the soy sauce and 4 tablespoons of the sugar in another small saucepan. Cook over medium heat until the sugar has dissolved. Add the fried tofu and simmer for 3 minutes. Remove from the heat and set aside.

Bring the dashi to the boil in a saucepan over medium–high heat. Add the remaining soy sauce and sugar and the mirin and adjust the heat so the mixture is simmering just below boiling point (or use Mentsuyu and warm water, see Tip).

Cook the udon noodles according to the packet instructions, then drain.

Gently reheat the fried tofu. Divide the cooked noodles among four deep bowls and pour in the warm dashi. Arrange the warm fried tofu and spring onions on top of the noodles and sprinkle with shichimi togarashi, if using.

COLD EGG NOODLE SALAD

冷やし中華

SERVES: 4 PREPARATION: 30 MINUTES COOKING: 20 MINUTES

FRESH

2 skinless chicken breast fillets,
   about 300 g (10½ oz)

3 Egg Crepes (see page 76)

2 tomatoes, halved lengthways
   and sliced

½ cucumber, cut into matchsticks

½ quantity of Miso Dressing
   (see page 100)

PANTRY

360 g (12¾ oz) dried egg noodles

30 g (1 oz) Pickled Ginger
   (see page 180), finely chopped,
   optional

This is a simple but satisfying lunch option that includes vegetables, meat, eggs and carbohydrates all in one dish. Try it with different toppings, such as prawns (shrimp), Soy-marinated Boiled Eggs (see page 76) or Tea-braised Pork (see page 138).

—

Place the chicken in a saucepan, cover with water and bring to the boil over medium heat. As soon as it reaches boiling point, turn off the heat and leave the chicken in the water for 15 minutes.

Cook the egg noodles according to the packet instructions, then drain and rinse under cold running water until cool.

When the chicken is cool enough to handle, remove it from the water and shred the meat.

Divide the noodles among four plates. Arrange the chicken, Egg Crepes, tomato and cucumber on top. Drizzle the dressing over the salad and serve sprinkled with the Pickled Ginger.

RAMEN

ラーメン

SERVES: 4 **PREPARATION:** *15 MINUTES* **COOKING:** *10 MINUTES*

FRESH

4 cups (1 litre) fresh chicken stock

90 ml (3 fl oz) Tea-braised Pork
    marinade (see page 138)

8 slices of Tea-braised Pork
    (see page 138)

2 Soy-marinated Boiled Eggs
    (see page 76), cut in half,
    or a plain soft-boiled egg

4 spring onions (scallions), white
    part only, cut into thin matchsticks
    and kept in ice-cold water

PANTRY

360 g (12¾ oz) dried egg noodles

This is a light, homemade version of ramen. If you want the full experience of a restaurant-style ramen meal, serve this with Karaage (see page 42), Gyoza (see page 54) and Crispy Garlic & Chilli Oil (see page 174).

—

Put the chicken stock and marinade in a large saucepan set over medium–high heat and bring to the boil. Keep warm.

Cook the egg noodles according to the packet instructions, then drain.

Divide the noodles among four large bowls. Arrange two slices of pork, half an egg and a quarter of the spring onion in each bowl and pour the soup over the top.

COLD UDON NOODLES WITH SESAME MISO SAUCE

冷やしうどんとゴマだれ

SERVES: 4 *PREPARATION: 10 MINUTES* *COOKING: 5 MINUTES*

FRESH

400 ml (14 fl oz) Basic Dashi Stock
(see page 204 or use powdered
dashi)

PANTRY

¼ cup (40 g) white sesame seeds

3 tablespoons light brown sugar

¼ cup (60 ml) red miso

2 tablespoons tahini

2¼ teaspoons soy sauce

1 kg (2 lb 4 oz) frozen udon noodles
or 400 g (14 oz) dried udon noodles

This creamy sesame sauce is so handy to have in the fridge as a
dressing for chicken salad or as a dipping sauce for vegetables.
If you want to prepare this in advance, you can omit the dashi
and add it just before serving, so that it will last longer (up to
a week in the fridge).

—

Gently toast the sesame seeds in a small frying pan over low
heat, shaking the pan from time to time to prevent burning.
As soon as you hear the sesame seeds popping, take the
pan off the heat and leave them to cool down.

Transfer the sesame seeds to a *suribachi* or mortar and coarsely
grind them.

Mix the sugar, miso, tahini, soy sauce, dashi and ground sesame
seeds in a bowl, stirring until the sugar has dissolved.

Cook the udon noodles according to the packet instructions,
then drain and rinse under cold running water until cool.

Divide the noodles among four plates. Serve the dipping sauce
in small individual bowls and dip the noodles into the sauce as
you eat them.

ZARU SOBA (SOBA NOODLES WITH SOY DIPPING SAUCE)

ざるそば

SERVES: 4 PREPARATION: 10 MINUTES COOKING: 5 MINUTES

FRESH

¾ cup (185 ml) Mentsuyu
(see page 212)

15 g (½ oz) fresh ginger,
peeled and finely grated

4 spring onions (scallions),
finely chopped

PANTRY

400 g (14 oz) soba noodles

2 teaspoons wasabi

2 tablespoons white sesame seeds,
toasted and coarsely ground

You can buy ready-made mentsuyu, but a homemade one is much cheaper and healthier, and so easy to make. It also keeps well – make a big batch so this dish can be prepared in minutes.

—

Cook the soba noodles according to the packet instructions, then drain and rinse under cold running water until cool.

Mix the mentsuyu with ½ cup (125 ml) cold water. Divide the noodles among four plates. Pour the mentsuyu into four small bowls for dipping.

Put the ginger, wasabi, spring onion and ground sesame seeds on smaller plates to be added according to taste to the diluted mentsuyu to make individual dipping sauces.

Dip a small amount of noodles into the sauce as you eat them.

DUCK SOBA NOODLES WITH HOT BROTH

鴨そば

SERVES: 4 PREPARATION: 15 MINUTES COOKING: 15 MINUTES

FRESH

12 spring onions (scallions),
    white part only

1.3 litres (45 fl oz) Basic Dashi Stock
    (see page 204 or use powdered
    dashi)

2 duck breasts, about 320 g (11¼ oz),
    thinly sliced on the diagonal

4 strips of organic, unwaxed lemon
    zest, each cut into 5 pieces

PANTRY

360 g (12¾ oz) soba noodles

¼ cup (60 ml) soy sauce

2 tablespoons mirin

2 teaspoons light brown sugar

shichimi togarashi (store-bought or
    homemade, see page 166), to serve

Tip: As an alternative to using the
dashi broth, soy sauce and sugar, you
could use 90 ml (3 fl oz) Mentsuyu
(see page 212) mixed with 1.3 litres
(45 fl oz) warm water instead.

This is a perfect quick meal for a cold day. The rich broth and
grilled spring onions will warm you up and the lemon zest
adds a little freshness to this noodle soup.

—

Heat a chargrill pan over high heat and grill the spring onions
for about 3–5 minutes, until they have grill marks. Turn them over
and cook on the other side. Remove from the pan and set aside.

Heat the dashi in a saucepan over medium–high heat. Add the soy
sauce, mirin and sugar and bring to the boil (or use Mentsuyu and
water, see Tip below).

Add the duck slices to the broth and cook for about 2–3 minutes,
until cooked through.

Meanwhile, cook the soba noodles according to the packet
instructions, then drain and divide among four bowls.

Pour the broth over the noodles. Arrange the duck and spring
onions on top, then add the lemon zest and sprinkle with shichimi
togarashi.

KYOTO-STYLE CURRIED BROTH WITH UDON NOODLES

京風カレーうどん

SERVES: 4 PREPARATION: 10 MINUTES COOKING: 15 MINUTES

FRESH

4 aburaage (thin, fried tofu)

1.2 litres (42 fl oz) Basic Dashi Stock (see page 204 or use powdered dashi), with an extra 2 g (1⁄16 oz) dashi powder added

16 spring onions (scallions), sliced into thick diagonal pieces

PANTRY

90 ml (3 fl oz) soy sauce

4 teaspoons light brown sugar

1 kg (2 lb 4 oz) frozen udon noodles or 400 g (14 oz) dried udon noodles

4 teaspoons mild curry powder

1⁄4 cup (35 g) arrowroot or cornflour (cornstarch)

This dish is called 'Kyoto-style' because it features two of Kyoto's specialty ingredients: dashi and *aburaage* (thin, fried tofu). Thickened curry broth and fried tofu combined with the sweetness of spring onions is happiness in a bowl.

—

Put the fried tofu in a colander. Pour boiling water over the tofu to remove the excess oil. Cut each piece of tofu into eight strips.

Heat the dashi in a saucepan over medium heat. Add the soy sauce and sugar and keep warm.

Cook the udon noodles according to the packet instructions, then drain.

Mix the curry powder, arrowroot and 75 ml (2¼ fl oz) water in a small bowl and stir until there are no lumps. Pour the mixture into the dashi and mix well. Simmer for 2 minutes, until the broth thickens. Add the noodles and sliced spring onion and cook until heated through.

Divide the broth and udon noodles among four bowls.

KAMATAMA UDON

釜玉うどん

SERVES: 4 PREPARATION: 10 MINUTES COOKING: 5 MINUTES

FRESH

4 egg yolks

4 spring onions, thinly sliced

¼ cup (60 ml) Mentsuyu (see page 212) or soy sauce

PANTRY

1 kg (2 lb 4 oz) frozen udon noodles or 360 g (12¾ oz) dried udon noodles

12 g (¼ oz) katsuobushi (dried bonito flakes)

This is a Japanese-style carbonara. In the Kagawa Prefecture, which is famous for udon noodles, there is a noodle shop on every corner, and this dish is served as a snack.

—

Make sure all the ingredients are prepared and ready before cooking the udon noodles.

Cook the udon noodles according to the packet instructions, then drain.

Quickly divide the hot noodles among four bowls. Top each with an egg yolk and a quarter of the spring onion and katsuobushi, and drizzle with the Mentsuyu or soy sauce. Serve immediately. Stir well with chopsticks as you eat.

CITRUS UDON

柑橘うどん

*SERVES: 4 **PREPARATION:** 10 MINUTES **COOKING:** 10 MINUTES*

FRESH

300 ml (10½ fl oz) ponzu (see page 216), chilled

300 ml (10½ fl oz) filtered water, chilled

2 organic, unwaxed limes, thinly sliced

PANTRY

¼ cup (40 g) white sesame seeds

1 kg (2 lb 4 oz) frozen udon noodles or 360 g (12¾ oz) dried udon noodles

Shop-bought ponzu tends to have a slightly harsher citrus flavour, so I recommend making it yourself for this particular recipe. It is a handy condiment to have in the fridge.

—

Gently toast the sesame seeds in a small frying pan over low heat, shaking the pan from time to time to prevent burning. As soon as you hear the sesame seeds popping, take the pan off the heat and leave them to cool down.

Transfer the sesame seeds to a *suribachi* or mortar and coarsely grind them.

Cook the udon noodles according to the packet instructions, then drain and rinse under cold running water until cool.

Divide the noodles among four bowls. Mix the chilled ponzu and water together, then pour it over the noodles. Sprinkle the ground sesame seeds over the top and arrange the lime slices over the noodles.

SMOKED MACKEREL & GINGER JAPANESE PILAF

鯖の炊き込みご飯

SERVES: 4 **PREPARATION:** *15 MINUTES, PLUS 1 HOUR STANDING* **COOKING:** *15 MINUTES*

FRESH

290 ml (10 fl oz) filtered water

50 g (1¾ oz) fresh ginger,
    peeled and cut into matchsticks

2 fillets of smoked mackerel,
    about 150 g (5½ oz), skin removed
    and flaked

2 spring onions (scallions),
    thinly sliced on the diagonal
    and kept in cold water

PANTRY

300 g (10½ oz) Japanese rice

2 tablespoons sake

1½ tablespoons soy sauce

1½ tablespoons mirin

We have a dried fish called *himono* in Japan, which is salted and traditionally dried in the sun. It has a concentrated umami flavour due to the drying process. Smoked mackerel is a good substitute, with some similarity in flavour and texture to *himono*.

—

Place the rice in a fine strainer and set it over a bowl of water. Gently stir and wash the rice with your hands. As soon as the water turns milky, lift the strainer and drain the water. Repeat this process three to four times until the water is less milky. Drain the rice and leave it to stand for 30 minutes.

Place the drained rice in a heavy-based saucepan (ideally, use a cast-iron pan). Add the filtered water, sake, soy sauce, mirin and 20 g (¾ oz) of the ginger, and cover with a tight-fitting lid.

Bring the rice to the boil over high heat. As soon as you hear the water boiling vigorously, reduce the heat to low and cook the rice for 11 minutes. Do not lift the lid while the rice is cooking – this is a strict rule! Remove the pan from the heat and leave to stand, covered, for 10 minutes.

Add the mackerel and remaining ginger to the rice. Gently mix together and fluff the rice. Cover the pan with a lid and set aside for 5 minutes for the mackerel to warm through. Serve with the shredded spring onion.

ONIGIRI
(RICE BALLS)

おにぎり

MAKES: 10 RICE BALLS **PREPARATION:** *20 MINUTES, PLUS 5–8 HOURS STANDING*
COOKING: *30 MINUTES*

FRESH

160 g (5½ oz) salmon fillet,
   skinned and pin-boned

5 g (⅛ oz) shiso (perilla) leaves or
   10 g (¼ oz) chives, finely chopped

PANTRY

2 teaspoons sea salt flakes

½ tablespoon sake

300 g (10½ oz) Japanese rice

1 tablespoon white sesame seeds,
   toasted

10 nori sheets

This is ideal for a work lunch or for a picnic – the ultimate bento box food! You can try this with different fillings and toppings. Use Pork Miso (see page 60), left-over Smoked Mackerel & Ginger Japanese Pilaf (see page 112), umeboshi (see page 16), Furikake (see page 176) or tuna mayonnaise.

—

Sprinkle a large pinch of sea salt on each side of the salmon. Drizzle the sake over the salmon and spread it over each side. Sprinkle salt over each side and massage it into the salmon. Leave the salmon for 5 hours or ideally overnight.

Cook the rice following the instructions on page 208.

Preheat the grill to medium–high. Pat the salmon dry (it will have released some liquid) and grill for 5 minutes on each side. Flake the cooked salmon.

When the rice is ready, add the flaked salmon, toasted sesame seeds and chopped shiso or chives to the pan. Mix with a moistened rice paddle so that the rice doesn't stick to it.

Sprinkle a small pinch of salt into your hand. Place about 80 g (2¾ oz) of the rice in your left hand and use your right hand to shape the rice into a pyramid. Wrap each onigiri in a nori sheet as you eat it. They're good eaten warm or cold.

Tip: If you find the shaping process too messy, you can use plastic wrap to help. Add ¼ teaspoon sea salt to the rice and mix well. Spread the plastic wrap on your work surface and put 80 g (2¾ oz) rice in the centre. You can either shape it into a pyramid or tightly twist the top to form a round onigiri.

JAPANESE-STYLE CURRY

カレーライス

SERVES: 4 **PREPARATION:** *30 MINUTES* **COOKING:** *50 MINUTES*

FRESH

1 large onion, thinly sliced

5 garlic cloves, grated

30 g (1 oz) fresh ginger, peeled
    and grated

4 skinless chicken thigh fillets,
    cut into bite-sized pieces

2 tablespoons butter

2 small apples, peeled and grated

2 carrots, coarsely grated

1 quantity of Steamed Rice
    (see page 208)

PANTRY

2 tablespoons sunflower oil

¼ cup (35 g) plain (all-purpose) flour

3 tablespoons mild curry powder

200 g (7 oz) tinned chopped tomatoes

1.2 litres (42 fl oz) good-quality
    chicken stock

2 tablespoons tomato sauce (ketchup)

3 tablespoons Worcestershire sauce

1½ teaspoons honey

3 tablespoons soy sauce

1 teaspoon sea salt

cornichons, tiny pickled onions and
    a soft-boiled egg, to serve, optional

The Japanese are experts at inventing their own versions of foreign dishes. They have a slight obsession with curry, so naturally they have created a Japanese version.

—

Heat the oil in a large, deep saucepan over low heat. Add the onion, garlic and ginger and cook until it turns a deep golden colour and begins to caramelise. Increase the heat to medium and stir-fry the mixture until the onion is golden.

Reduce the heat, add the chicken and fry for 3 minutes. Add the butter and flour and stir for 2 minutes. Add the curry powder, then increase the heat and cook until aromatic. Add the chopped tomatoes and cook for 5 minutes.

Add 1 cup (250 ml) of the stock and mix well. Pour in the rest of the stock, then add the tomato sauce, Worcestershire sauce, honey, soy sauce, apple and carrot. Bring to the boil, then reduce the heat. Simmer for 30 minutes, stirring occasionally to prevent burning. Add the salt, to taste.

Scoop the rice into bowls and spoon the curry on top. Serve with the cornichons, pickled onions and a soft-boiled egg, if using.

MAIN MEALS

NANBANZUKE (MARINATED SALMON)

南蛮漬け

SERVES: 4 *PREPARATION: 30 MINUTES* *COOKING: 20 MINUTES*

FRESH

300 ml (10½ fl oz) Basic Dashi Stock (see page 204 or use powdered dashi)

3 tablespoons freshly squeezed lemon juice

500 g (1 lb 2 oz) salmon fillets, cut into 1.5 cm (⅝ inch) slices

1 onion, thinly sliced

1 carrot, cut into thin matchsticks

1 red and 1 green capsicum (pepper), thinly sliced

PANTRY

¾ cup (185 ml) rice vinegar

2½ tablespoons soy sauce

4½ tablespoons mirin

1½ tablespoons sake

1½ tablespoons light brown sugar

sea salt and ground black pepper

¼ cup (30 g) cornflour (cornstarch) or potato flour

90 ml (3 fl oz) sunflower oil

This is the perfect meal for a summer gathering and it can be served as a starter or a main. You can prepare it a day in advance and it will taste even better the next day.

—

First, prepare the marinade. Combine the dashi, vinegar, soy sauce, mirin, sake and sugar in a saucepan. Place over medium heat and cook until almost boiling, then remove from the heat and leave to cool. Add the lemon juice to the cooled marinade.

Season the salmon with salt and pepper and lightly coat with the cornflour.

Heat half the oil in a frying pan over medium heat and fry the salmon in batches until crispy. Lift from the pan with tongs, and shake to remove any excess oil. Place the fried salmon directly into the marinade while the salmon is still warm. Repeat until you have finished frying all the fish.

Wipe the pan with paper towel to remove any left-over oil. Heat the remaining oil over medium heat. Cook the onion for 1 minute, then add the carrot and cook for 1 minute. Add the capsicum and cook for 2–3 minutes, until the vegetables are cooked but still have a slight crunch. Transfer the vegetables directly to the marinade with the salmon.

This dish can be served immediately or chilled. The flavours will develop when chilled and marinated for a couple of hours or overnight. Store in the fridge for up to 3 days.

TEMPURA
天ぷら

SERVES: 4 PREPARATION: 25 MINUTES COOKING: 20 MINUTES

FRESH

1 egg, chilled

150 ml (5 fl oz) ice-cold sparkling water

4 large king prawns (shrimp), peeled and deveined, tails on

240 g (8½ oz) kabocha or butternut pumpkin (squash) or sweet potato, cut into 5 mm (¼ inch) half-moon slices

8 Padrón peppers or 8 shiso (perilla) leaves, optional

4 large shiitake mushrooms, scored with a cross on the caps

PANTRY

160 g (5½ oz) self-raising flour, chilled

3 cups (750 ml) sunflower oil, for deep-frying

a pinch of sea salt

Tempura is fantastic served with a dipping sauce of warm Mentsuyu (see page 212) – dilute 1½ tablespoons mentsuyu with 2 tablespoons hot water. Alternatively, try it with a tea-flavoured salt (see page 172).

—

Before you start, make sure that the egg and flour are chilled in the fridge and that your sparkling water is ice cold.

Heat the sunflower oil in a deep saucepan over medium heat. Preheat the oven to 100°C (200°F).

Crack the egg into a large bowl, add the sparkling water and salt and beat with a whisk. Sift the flour into the bowl and whisk very lightly. Don't worry if you have unmixed dry flour in the mixture. The consistency should be like single cream.

When the oil reaches 180°C (350°F), dip two or three of the ingredients into the batter at a time – the prawns and pumpkin can be completely dipped into the batter, but the peppers, shiso leaves and mushrooms should only be dipped on one side.

Gently slide the battered ingredients into the oil and fry for about 2 minutes for each batch, until the batter becomes crispy. Lift the tempura out using tongs, shake them a few times to remove any excess oil, then drain on paper towel.

Serve the tempura as you cook it or place it in the oven to keep warm. Serve with warm broth or sea salt.

SASHIMI

刺身

SERVES: 4 *PREPARATION: 20 MINUTES*

FRESH

600 g (1 lb 5 oz) salmon, tuna
    or yellowtail fillet, skin and
    bones removed

200 g (7 oz) daikon radish, peeled,
    finely shredded with a mandolin
    and kept in cold water

4 shiso (perilla) leaves

PANTRY

wasabi and soy sauce, to serve

Tip: It's best to use a long, sharp knife
for making sashimi.

The key to making good sashimi is to purchase the freshest
piece of fish possible. The best option is to ask your fishmonger
for the freshest that day. If you are making sashimi from a
bigger fish, such as tuna or salmon, it's a good idea to ask for
the loin of the fish, which is referred to as the *saku* in Japanese.

—

Place the fish on a chopping board, with the side that had skin
attached facing up.

Place the bottom edge of the knife blade against the sashimi
and cut it into 1 cm (½ inch) slices with one clean stroke, while
pulling the knife towards you. Try not to saw the sashimi.

Drain the daikon.

Neatly arrange the drained daikon, shiso leaves, wasabi and
sashimi on a plate. Serve with a little dish of soy sauce on the
side for dipping.

YUZU-MARINATED SALMON
サーモンの柚子マリネ

SERVES: 4 AS A STARTER **PREPARATION:** *10 MINUTES, PLUS 8 HOURS STANDING*

FRESH

200 g (7 oz) salmon fillet, skin
  and bones removed

½ onion

100 g (3½ oz) daikon radish, peeled,
  or 8 French radishes

3 teaspoons yuzu juice (or
  1½ teaspoons lemon juice mixed
  with 1½ teaspoons orange juice)

5 g (⅛ oz) grated lemon zest

PANTRY

1 teaspoon light brown sugar

2 teaspoons sea salt

2 tablespoons extra virgin olive oil

2 teaspoons soy sauce

shichimi togarashi (store-bought
  or homemade, see page 166), optional

You can prepare this dish well ahead of time. The citrus flavour goes well with the richness of the salmon, and the fresh crunch of the thinly sliced daikon and onion add a lovely texture. This is a perfect light meal for a summer afternoon.

—

Cut the salmon fillet in half lengthways along the backbone line. Sprinkle the sugar and salt on both sides of the salmon, wrap in plastic wrap and keep in the fridge overnight.

Thinly slice the onion and daikon and place in a bowl of ice-cold water until ready to serve.

Mix the yuzu juice, olive oil and soy sauce in a small bowl.

Slice the salmon fillet with a sharp knife (see page 124).

Arrange the salmon on a plate. Drain the onion and daikon and pat dry with paper towel. Scatter the vegetables over the salmon and sprinkle with the lemon zest. Drizzle the yuzu dressing over the top and sprinkle with shichimi togarashi, if using.

NIGIRI SUSHI

握り寿司

MAKES: ABOUT 40-50 NIGIRI **PREPARATION:** *45 MINUTES*

FRESH

400 g (14 oz) salmon, tuna
  or yellowtail fillet, skin and
  bones removed

4 scallops

1 quantity of cooked Sushi Rice,
  cooled to room temperature
  (see page 210)

50 g (1¾ oz) salmon caviar

PANTRY

1 teaspoon rice vinegar

2 teaspoons wasabi

soy sauce, for dipping

Tip: For best results, avoid using
cold rice.

Making nigiri sushi is easier than you think. The key is to purchase the freshest fish possible and to cut it using the correct technique (see page 124). Follow the sushi rice instructions on page 210 for the perfect rice.

—

Following the instructions on page 124, slice the fish into 5 cm (2 inch) long, 3 cm (1¼ inch) wide and 1 cm (½ inch) thick slices. Slice the scallops in half, without cutting all the way through, then open out flat like a book.

Add the rice vinegar to a small bowl of water and put some wasabi in a tiny dish. Wet both of your hands with the water – this will prevent the rice from sticking to your hands.

Scoop 20 g (¾ oz) sushi rice into your right hand and gently shape it to make a long oval shape. Try to not grip it too hard so the rice holds its own shape. Flatten the base of the rice. The top, which is where the fish will lay, should be rounder in shape.

Spread a small amount of wasabi onto the sashimi. Gently lay the sashimi on top of the rice, wasabi side down, and lightly press so the sashimi sticks to the rice. Repeat until all the rice and sashimi has been used.

Garnish the sushi with the caviar and serve with the soy sauce for dipping.

TEMAKI SUSHI
(DIY HAND-ROLLED SUSHI)

手巻き寿司

SERVES: 4-6 **PREPARATION:** *30 MINUTES*

FRESH

2 quantities of cooked Sushi Rice,
   cooled to room temperature
   (see page 210)

600–800 g (1 lb 5 oz–1 lb 12 oz) mixture
   of your favourite sashimi – yellowtail,
   salmon, sea bream, tuna or cured
   mackerel fillets (see page 150),
   boiled prawns (shrimp), crab and
   salmon caviar are all good options
   (see page 124 for cutting sashimi)

½ cucumber, cut into thin strips

1 avocado, peeled and sliced

shiso (perilla) leaves or baby cress,
   to serve

PANTRY

2 nori sheets, cut into quarters

wasabi and soy sauce, to serve

This is a fantastic way to share food with your friends and family. All you need to do is prepare plenty of sushi rice and purchase the best-quality ingredients you can afford. There's no hard work involved, yet it's an impressive meal, and people love making their own sushi.

—

Have a nori sheet in your hand and put 2 tablespoons sushi rice on top. Top with 2–3 fillings, such as salmon, avocado and shiso.

Wrap the nori around the rice and filling to form a cornet shape, or simply fold it in half.

Dip the sushi into some soy sauce, then pop it into your mouth and repeat!

There are no strict rules on what to use for fillings. Be creative and make your own favourite combinations: tuna mayonnaise, Miso Pork (see page 60), Teriyaki Chicken (see page 90) and Rolled Omelette (see page 34) are all child-friendly options. Thin strips of Teriyaki Tofu Steak (see page 52) is a great option for vegetarians.

HOSOMAKI (THIN SUSHI ROLLS)

細巻き

MAKES: 24 PIECES **PREPARATION:** *30 MINUTES*

FRESH

320 g (11¼ oz) cooked Sushi Rice, cooled to room temperature (see page 210)

120 g (4¼ oz) cucumber, avocado or pin-boned salmon fillet, cut into 1 cm (½ inch) thick strips

PANTRY

2 nori sheets, cut in half lengthways

wasabi and soy sauce, to serve

If you don't have a sushi mat, don't worry – a clean tea towel will also work for this sushi. You can try lots of different fillings, such as cucumber, avocado, tuna, etc.

—

Prepare a small bowl of water to wet your fingers when handling the sushi rice to avoid it sticking.

Place the halved nori sheets, shiny side down, on the bottom end of a sushi mat.

Wet your fingers with water and spread 80 g (2¾ oz) of the sushi rice evenly on the nori, leaving a 1 cm (½ inch) border along the top edge.

Lay a strip of cucumber, avocado or salmon along the middle of the rice.

Let's roll! Lift the corners of the bottom of the sushi mat with your fingers and roll over the filling. The bottom of the nori should meet with the top border of the rice and tighten the roll.

Unroll the sushi mat, moisten the empty border of nori with a little water and seal and tighten again with the mat. Repeat with the rest of the rice and filling.

Place the roll of sushi on a chopping board and moisten a sharp knife. Cut the roll in the middle. Put the two halves side by side, and cut again and again so that you have eight equal pieces. Slice the rest of the rolls in the same way.

Serve with wasabi and soy sauce for dipping.

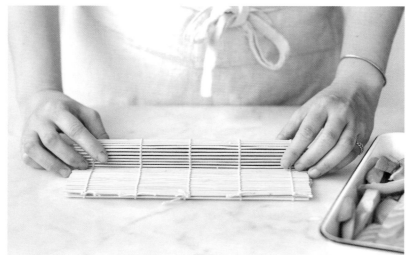

INARI SUSHI (TOFU SUSHI POCKET)

いなり寿司

MAKES: 20 PIECES PREPARATION: 1 HOUR COOKING: 20 MINUTES

FRESH

20 aburaage (thin, fried tofu)

1 quantity of cooked Sushi Rice,
    cooled to room temperature
    (see page 210)

150 g (5½ oz) shelled edamame,
    blanched in boiling water for
    2 minutes, then cooled in cold water

30 g (1 oz) Pickled Ginger
    (see page 180), thinly sliced

PANTRY

1½ tablespoons soy sauce

1 tablespoon light brown sugar

1 tablespoon black or white sesame
    seeds, toasted

Make sure you use the square-shaped *aburaage* (thin, fried tofu), rather than rectangular-shaped ones for inari sushi, otherwise you will have a lot of wasted tofu.

—

Cut each piece of tofu in half to make two rectangular pieces. Carefully open the cut side so as not to break it.

Bring a saucepan of water to the boil over high heat, then reduce the heat to low. Add the tofu and cook for 2 minutes to remove the excess oil. Drain and leave to cool, then gently squeeze the tofu to remove any excess liquid.

Mix the soy sauce, sugar and 75 ml (2¼ fl oz) water in a jug. Arrange the prepared tofu in a large frying pan and pour the soy sauce mixture over the top. Simmer over medium–low heat for 5 minutes, until the tofu has absorbed most of the sauce. Leave the tofu to cool in the pan.

While the tofu is cooling, mix the sushi rice, sesame seeds, edamame and pickled ginger together in a bowl.

Spoon 40 g (1½ oz) of the rice mixture into one of the cooled tofu pockets and stand it upright. Repeat until all of the tofu and rice have been used.

HOTPOT

鍋

SERVES: 4 PREPARATION: 20 MINUTES COOKING: 10 MINUTES

FRESH

600 g (1 lb 5 oz) pork belly, thinly
  sliced, or a boneless chicken thigh,
  cut into bite-sized pieces (fish like
  salmon or cod, and tofu can also
  be used)

¼ Chinese cabbage (wong bok),
  cut into bite-sized pieces

1 leek or 1 bunch spring onions
  (scallions), sliced

300 g (10½ oz) mixed mushrooms,
  such as sliced shiitake, enoki
  and shimeji

¼ daikon radish, grated

PANTRY

10 cm (4 inch) square piece of kombu
  (dried kelp), optional

ponzu (store-bought or homemade,
  see page 216), for dipping

shichimi togarashi (store-bought or
  homemade, see page 166), to serve

This is another 'no hard work involved' meal that's meant for
sharing. You'll need a camping hotplate or a tabletop electric
hotplate, which you can purchase online – they're inexpensive
and a handy tool to have around the kitchen. Try serving this
with the Miso Dressing (see page 168) as a dipping sauce.

—

Soak the kombu in 4 cups (1 litre) of water in a shallow casserole
dish (ideally, use a Japanese donabe pan if you have one – make
sure that the pan you use isn't too shallow for frying).

Pour the ponzu into four shallow bowls for dipping.

Set a camping hotplate or tabletop electric hotplate in the middle of
your table and bring the water to the boil in the casserole dish, then
turn the heat down to a simmer. Add one-quarter of the ingredients,
cover and cook for 2 minutes or until the meat is cooked.

Open the lid of the casserole and invite each person to pick up
the food using chopsticks and dunk the food in the dipping sauce
as they eat. Add grated daikon radish and shichimi togarashi as
desired. When each batch is finished, cook another batch.

TEA-BRAISED PORK

紅茶豚

SERVES: 6-8 **PREPARATION:** *5 MINUTES, PLUS 8 HOURS CHILLING* **COOKING:** *2-3 HOURS*

FRESH

900 g (2 lb) pork belly, skin and
bones removed, and rolled

2 garlic cloves, sliced

PANTRY

2 English Breakfast teabags

1½ cups (375 ml) soy sauce

⅔ cup (170 ml) sake

⅔ cup (170 ml) mirin

2 tablespoons light brown sugar

This pork is amazing served cold with Japanese or English
mustard. It can also be served on salad, or cubed and used
in fried rice. However, I think it's best when served on top of
ramen noodles (see page 98).

—

Place the pork and tea in a large saucepan and cover with
water. Bring to the boil, then reduce the heat to low and
simmer for about 2-3 hours, until the pork is soft.

Combine the soy sauce, sake, mirin and sugar in a small
saucepan over high heat and bring to the boil. Remove
from the heat immediately and add the sliced garlic.

Put the pork in a large container and pour the sauce over
the top. Cover and chill overnight before using. The pork
will keep in the fridge for up to 1 week in an airtight container
as long as the meat is covered by the sauce while it is stored.

BEEF TATAKI (SEARED BEEF FILLET)

牛肉のたたき

SERVES: 4 PREPARATION: 20 MINUTES COOKING: 5 MINUTES

FRESH

400 g (14 oz) good-quality beef
    fillet tail

¼ cup (60 ml) orange juice

1 garlic clove, crushed with the back
    of a knife but left whole

1 onion, thinly sliced and kept
    in cold water

2 cups (60 g) watercress, washed

200 g (7 oz) daikon radish,
    finely grated, optional

PANTRY

sea salt and ground black pepper

2 tablespoons mirin

2 tablespoons sake

¼ cup (60 ml) soy sauce

2 tablespoons rice vinegar

This is a super-easy, delicious meal for entertaining. The key is using the tail of a beef fillet, which is thinner (and much cheaper), so it will cook very quickly. This recipe will also work well with sirloin steak.

—

Take the beef out of the fridge and bring it to room temperature. Season with sea salt and pepper.

To make the sauce, gently heat the mirin and sake in a small saucepan. Remove from the heat and add the soy sauce, vinegar, orange juice and crushed garlic.

Heat a frying pan over medium–high heat. Sear the beef for about 1–2 minutes on all sides. Remove from the heat and leave the beef to rest for at least 10 minutes.

Drain the onion and combine with the watercress on a serving plate. Cut the beef into 5 mm (¼ inch) thick slices and add to the salad. Serve with the sauce drizzled over the top. Drain any excess liquid from the grated daikon, and add it to the salad just before serving.

Tip: You could make a larger batch of sauce and keep it in a clean screw-top jar for up to 2 weeks in the fridge.

KUSHIKATSU
(CRISPY PORK SKEWERS)

串カツ

SERVES: 4 PREPARATION: 40 MINUTES COOKING: 20 MINUTES

FRESH

600 g (1 lb 5 oz) pork shoulder steak

½ large onion, cut into 4 wedges

4 okra, stems trimmed

2 eggs, lightly beaten with a pinch
   of salt

tonkatsu sauce (store-bought or
   homemade, see page 214), to serve

PANTRY

8 wooden skewers, soaked in water
   for 30 minutes

½ cup (75 g) plain (all-purpose) flour
   mixed with a pinch of salt
   and pepper

1⅔ cups (100 g) panko breadcrumbs

2 cups (500 ml) sunflower oil,
   for deep-frying

Osaka is famous for its *kushikatsu* and has hundreds of casual standing bars that specialise in it. Their menus are endless because so many different kinds of meat and vegetables can be skewered and panko-crusted. The customers share big bowls of dipping sauce and the restaurants have signs that say 'Strictly no double-dipping' for health and safety reasons!

—

Cut the pork steak into 2 x 9 cm (¾ x 3½ inch) strips. Using two skewers at a time, skewer the ingredients in this order: pork, onion, pork, okra, pork (one kushikatsu is made from two skewers – after cooking, it is cut through the middle to make two individual kushikatsu skewers).

Preheat the oven to 100°C (200°F).

Place the flour, beaten eggs and breadcrumbs in three separate shallow trays. Dip the skewers into the flour first, coat evenly, then pat off any excess flour. Next, dip the skewers in the egg. Finally, carefully cover the skewers with breadcrumbs.

Heat the sunflower oil in a deep saucepan over high heat to 180°C (350°F). Fry two kushikatsu at once for about 4 minutes, until the crust becomes golden and crispy. Lift out with tongs or a large slotted spoon and drain on paper towel. Keep the kushikatsu warm in the oven while you continue cooking.

When all the skewers are done, cut in between the skewers to make eight half-skewers. Serve with tonkatsu sauce for dipping.

MISO-MARINATED SALMON

鮭の西京味噌

SERVES: 4 PREPARATION: 15 MINUTES, PLUS 30 MINUTES STANDING
AND 8 HOURS MARINATING COOKING: 10 MINUTES

FRESH

4 salmon fillets with skin on,
   pin-boned, about 120 g (4¼ oz) each

PANTRY

½ teaspoon sea salt

2 tablespoons saikyo miso
   (sweet white miso)

3 tablespoons mirin

1½ tablespoons sake

2 teaspoons caster (superfine) sugar

This miso marinade can be kept in the fridge and re-used
two to three times with different ingredients. Recognising
the variety of miso can be quite confusing. *Saikyo miso* is an
extra-sweet white miso and tastes a little like salty custard.
Don't confuse it with regular white miso as it is much saltier
(see page 20 for more information about miso).

—

Sprinkle salt on both sides of the salmon fillets and leave them
in the fridge for 30 minutes.

Mix the miso, mirin, sake and sugar and pour this mixture
into a small non-metallic tray or a resealable plastic bag.

Pat the salmon fillets dry with paper towel, then add them to
the miso marinade. Marinate the fish in the fridge overnight
or for up to 4 days – the flavour will get stronger the longer
it marinates.

Preheat the grill to medium–high.

Lift the salmon from the marinade and completely remove
the marinade using paper towel. Cook the salmon under the
hot grill for 4 minutes on each side, keeping a careful eye on
it as the miso marinade tends to burn easily.

CHIRASHI SUSHI

ちらし寿司

SERVES: 4-5 **PREPARATION:** *40 MINUTES, 1½ HOURS SOAKING* **COOKING:** *10 MINUTES*

FRESH

80 g (2¾ oz) carrot, cut into
   thin matchsticks

80 g (2¾ oz) snow peas (mangetout),
   thinly sliced

2 quantities of cooked Sushi Rice,
   cooled to room temperature
   (see page 210)

2 quantities of Egg Crepes
   (see page 76), shredded

200 g (7 oz) of your favourite sashimi,
   such as salmon or yellowtail
   (see page 124)

50 g (1¾ oz) salmon caviar, optional

Pickled Ginger (see page 180), to serve

PANTRY

20 g (¾ oz) dried shiitake mushrooms
   (about 8 whole dried mushrooms)

2 tablespoons soy sauce, plus extra
   for dipping

2 teaspoons light brown sugar

2 tablespoons white sesame seeds,
   toasted

This is an impressive celebratory meal, with toppings varying depending on the region and the family's traditions. It can be prepared in advance and makes a perfect party dish.

—

Soak the dried shiitake in a bowl of hot water for 1½ hours, or in room temperature water overnight. Drain (reserve the soaking water as it makes a nice broth). Remove the stalks and thinly slice the caps.

Place the sliced shiitake in a frying pan with the soy sauce and sugar and simmer for 2 minutes over medium heat. Add the carrot and snow peas and cook for 2 minutes. Remove from the heat and leave to cool.

Add the cooled vegetable mixture and the sesame seeds to the sushi rice and combine well.

Place the rice on a large platter and cover with the shredded egg crepes. Arrange the sashimi on top and add the salmon caviar, if using. Serve with pickled ginger and small dishes of soy sauce for the sashimi.

Tips: If you are preparing this in advance, prepare it up until the stage that calls for you to combine the vegetable mixture, sesame seeds and rice. Add all of the toppings just before serving. Do not keep the rice in the fridge as that hardens the rice.

SWEET SOY-SIMMERED PORK BELLY & EGG

豚の角煮

SERVES: 4 PREPARATION: 10 MINUTES COOKING: 1 HOUR 50 MINUTES

FRESH

1 kg (2 lb 4 oz) pork belly, skin
    and bone removed, cut into
    4 cm (1½ inch) cubes

2 spring onions (scallions),
    cut in half

2 garlic cloves, crushed with the
    back of a knife but left whole

3 cm (1¼ inch) piece of fresh
    ginger, peeled, thinly sliced
    and finely shredded

4 eggs, at room temperature

PANTRY

75 ml (2¼ fl oz) soy sauce

¼ cup (60 ml) sake

3 tablespoons light brown sugar

Japanese or English mustard,
    to serve, optional

This slow-braised pork is a great winter meal. It is a little time-consuming, but is definitely worth the effort. It's lovely with a strong Japanese or English mustard, or with Yuzu Kosho (see page 170).

—

Place the pork belly in a large saucepan with the spring onions, garlic and half the ginger. Cover with water and bring to the boil, then reduce the heat to medium–low and cook for 1 hour. Skim off the fat and scum from the surface as it cooks.

Bring a small saucepan of water to the boil, then reduce the heat to medium. Gently drop the eggs into the water and cook for 8 minutes. Drain the water and cool the eggs by running them under cold water. Leave the eggs in cold water to cool, then peel.

Remove the saucepan of pork from the heat. Use tongs to lift the pork into another large saucepan. Add the soy sauce, sake, sugar and the remaining ginger. Pour the pork cooking liquid over the pork in the new pan to cover the meat.

Place the pan over medium heat and bring to the boil, then reduce the heat and simmer for 30 minutes. Add the boiled eggs 10 minutes before serving to warm them through.

You can serve the pork and egg straight away, but for the best flavour, leave it to cool completely and reheat it one more time. This helps the pork to absorb even more sauce. Serve with mustard, if liked.

CURED MACKEREL-PRESSED SUSHI

鯖寿司

MAKES: 16 PREPARATION: 30 MINUTES, PLUS 1 HOUR SALTING AND 40 MINUTES MARINATING
COOKING: 15 MINUTES

FRESH

2 large fresh mackerel fillets, about
    150 g (5½ oz) each – ask your
    fishmonger to fillet and pin-bone
    it for you

6–8 shiso (perilla) leaves, optional

1 quantity of cooked Sushi Rice,
    cooled to room temperature
    (see page 210)

PANTRY

15 g (½ oz) sea salt

10 cm (4 inch) square piece of kombu
    (dried kelp)

300 ml (10½ fl oz) rice vinegar
    (or enough to cover the fillets)

soy sauce, to serve

The central city of Kyoto is located in an inland area. Before transportation systems were developed, it was hard to get fresh fish, such as mackerel. This sushi was born in the days when mackerel needed to be preserved in salt for shipping.

—

Salt the mackerel fillets on both sides, place them in a tray and refrigerate for 1 hour. Quickly rinse the mackerel fillets in a bowl of water (the flesh of the fish is delicate, so don't wash it under running water). Pat the mackerel dry with paper towel.

Place the mackerel fillets in a deep tray and top with the kombu. Pour in enough vinegar so that the fish is just covered. Marinate for 20 minutes, then flip the fillets over and marinate for a further 20 minutes (you can marinate the fish for up to 3 hours, depending on how pickled you want it to be).

Pat the mackerel dry and place it on a chopping board, skin side up. Carefully peel off the film-like layer of skin, keeping the thicker skin intact.

Line a sushi mat with a sheet of plastic wrap and lay one of the fillets, flesh side up, in the middle of the mat. Lay half the shiso leaves on top, if using, then shape half the rice into a log to sit along the inside of the fillet. Lift the mat to roll the sushi and shape firmly so that the rice and fish stick together. Unroll the mat and repeat with the second fish fillet.

Cut each mackerel fillet into eight to ten equal pieces and serve with soy sauce.

TONKATSU
(JAPANESE PORK CUTLET)
とんかつ

SERVES: 4 PREPARATION: 30 MINUTES COOKING: 15 MINUTES

FRESH

4 pork loin steaks, about 170 g (5¾ oz) each, skin and bones removed

2 eggs, lightly beaten

400 g (14 oz) soft white cabbage (about ¼ small cabbage), shredded and kept in ice-cold water

½ cup (125 ml) Quick Tonkatsu Sauce (see page 214)

PANTRY

sea salt and ground black pepper

¼ cup (35 g) plain (all-purpose) flour

2 cups (120 g) panko breadcrumbs

2 cups (500 ml) sunflower oil, for deep-frying

Tonkatsu is one of the most popular *yo-syoku* dishes (Western-influenced Japanese cuisine). I recommend preparing the pork using a meat tenderiser, which is a great kitchen tool to have. You can also try katsu sandwiches – spread butter on toast and sandwich the katsu and tonkatsu sauce inside with shredded cabbage. Heavenly!

—

Bring the pork steaks to room temperature. If you have thick steaks, make five or six incisions where the meat meets the fat on both sides. This will tenderise the pork and prevent it from curling during cooking. Season with salt and black pepper.

Place the flour, beaten eggs and breadcrumbs in three separate shallow bowls. Coat the pork in the flour first and pat to remove any excess flour. Next, dip the pork into the egg. Finally, cover the pork with breadcrumbs. (You can freeze the coated pork at this stage if needed.)

Heat the sunflower oil in a deep saucepan to 180°C (350°F). Cook two pork steaks for about 3 minutes, until golden brown. Use a metal strainer to remove the tonkatsu and place on paper towel to drain. Repeat with the rest of the steaks, then fry each tonkatsu again for another minute and drain on paper towel.

Drain the cabbage completely.

Cut the tonkatsu into thin slices. Serve with the cabbage and drizzle with the tonkatsu sauce.

EBI FRY
(PANKO-CRUSTED FRIED PRAWN)

海老フライ

SERVES: 4 PREPARATION: 30 MINUTES COOKING: 20 MINUTES

FRESH

2 hard-boiled eggs, peeled
  and chopped

12 large tiger prawns (shrimp),
  peeled and deveined, tails on

2 eggs, lightly beaten

PANTRY

2 tablespoons mayonnaise

50 g (1¾ oz) cornichons,
  finely chopped

50 g (1¾ oz) small pickled onions,
  finely chopped

a large pinch of sea salt

⅔ cup (100 g) plain (all-purpose) flour

1⅔ cups (100 g) panko breadcrumbs

3 cups (750 ml) sunflower oil,
  for deep-frying

These crispy panko-crusted prawns are a firm favourite with kids and adults, so make them for a special meal with family and friends. They're commonly served with tartare sauce, but are also great served with Quick Tonkatsu Sauce (see page 214).

—

To prepare the tartare sauce, mix the mayonnaise, cornichons, pickled onions and chopped hard-boiled eggs together.

Place the prawns in a small bowl and cover with water. Add the salt and leave them for 10 minutes.

Place the flour, beaten eggs and breadcrumbs in three separate shallow dishes. Dust the prawns with flour, then dip them in the egg. Finally, coat the prawns with the breadcrumbs.

Heat the sunflower oil in a large deep saucepan or wok to 180°C (350°F). Fry the prawns, four at a time, for about 2–3 minutes, until golden brown. Lift the prawns out of the oil with a metal strainer and place them on paper towel to drain.

Serve with the tartare sauce.

SEA BREAM CARPACCIO

鯛のカルパッチョ

SERVES: 4 AS AN APPETISER **PREPARATION:** *20 MINUTES*

FRESH

2 sea bream fillets, about 100 g
(3½ oz) each, skin removed – ask
your fishmonger to pin-bone them
for you

2 teaspoons Yuzu Kosho (store-bought
or homemade, see page 170)

1 cup (60 g) alfalfa sprouts

2 French radishes, thinly sliced

PANTRY

1½ teaspoons toasted sesame oil

1 teaspoon sea salt

Sea bream has a perfect balance of delicate sweetness and
richness and is a fantastic fish for sashimi (see page 124).
Yuzu Kosho is a key ingredient for this recipe – it's a useful
condiment to have and can be found in many Japanese stores.

—

Cut the sea bream fillets in half along the middle line so that you
have four pieces. Cut the pieces into 3 mm (⅛ inch) thick sashimi
slices (see page 124).

Arrange the sliced sea bream on a plate and use a cocktail stick
or chopsticks to put a tiny amount of yuzu kosho on the sashimi.
Drizzle the sesame oil over the fish and sprinkle with the salt.

Scatter the alfalfa sprouts and radishes over the dish.

CONDIMENTS

JAPANESE ONION DRESSING

オニオンドレッシング

MAKES: 300 ML (10½ FL OZ) PREPARATION: 10 MINUTES COOKING: 3 MINUTES

FRESH

2 small onions, finely chopped

1 garlic clove

PANTRY

75 ml (2½ fl oz) extra virgin olive oil

¼ cup (60 ml) soy sauce

¼ cup (60 ml) rice vinegar

2 teaspoons light brown sugar

2 cm (¾ inch) piece of fresh ginger, peeled

This flavour-packed dressing is not only delicious on a salad (such as the Tofu, Tomato and Shiso Salad on page 68 and the Chicory Salad on page 72), but is also fantastic as a marinade for steak, grilled fish and grilled vegetables.

—

Heat 1 tablespoon of the olive oil in a frying pan over medium heat and cook the onion for 3 minutes.

Place the cooked onion, the remaining olive oil, soy sauce, rice vinegar, sugar, ginger and garlic in a blender and blitz until well blended.

Store the dressing in a sterilised screw-top jar and keep refrigerated for up to 10 days.

NAMETAKE
(ENOKI IN SOY SAUCE)

なめたけ

MAKES: ABOUT 200 ML (7 FL OZ) **PREPARATION:** *10 MINUTES* **COOKING:** *10 MINUTES*

FRESH

200 g (7 oz) enoki mushrooms

PANTRY

2½ tablespoons soy sauce

3 tablespoons sake

2½ teaspoons light brown sugar

1¼ tablespoons mirin

2.5 cm (1 inch) square piece of kombu
(dried kelp), cut into 2 mm (¹⁄₁₆ inch)
thin strips

Nametake is one of the staple preserved foods that Japanese people always have in their fridge. It is most commonly eaten with a side dish of rice but is also used as a condiment or sauce. *Nametake* is delicious when served with chilled silken tofu or grated daikon radish. Also try it with Zaru Soba (see page 102) or Citrus Udon (see page 110).

—

Cut 2.5 cm (1 inch) off the bottom part of the mushrooms, then cut them in half across the middle.

Place all the ingredients in a saucepan with 2½ tablespoons water. Cook over medium–low heat until just below boiling point.

Reduce the heat to low and cook until the juices slightly thicken. Place in a sterilised screw-top jar and store in the fridge for up to a week.

SHICHIMI TOGARASHI (SEVEN SPICE MIX)

七味唐辛子

MAKES: A 50 ML (1½ FL OZ) JAR **PREPARATION:** *10 MINUTES* **COOKING:** *10 MINUTES*

FRESH

three 1 x 5 cm (½ x 2 inch) pieces of orange peel, white pith removed

two 1 x 5 cm (½ x 2 inch) peeled slices of fresh ginger

PANTRY

1 tablespoon chilli flakes

½ teaspoon sansho Japanese pepper or whole black peppercorns

1 tablespoon black or white sesame seeds

½ tablespoon white or black poppy seeds

1 teaspoon aonori powder or nori flakes

Shichimi togarashi is a Japanese spice mix that is a blend of seven ingredients, such as chilli flakes, herbs, spices and seeds – the ingredients and proportions vary, depending on the brand. It gives an extra spicy kick to your meal. Try it with Lotus Root Crisps (see page 30) or Agedashi Tofu (see page 78).

—

Put the orange peel and ginger on a baking tray and leave it at room temperature for half a day, or dry it in a 170°C (340°F) oven for 5–7 minutes.

Blitz the dried orange peel and ginger in a spice grinder or a mini food processor.

Coarsely grind the chilli flakes, pepper and half the sesame seeds in a mortar and pestle.

Mix all the ingredients together and store in a sterilised screw-top jar for up to 2–3 months.

MISO

01. INSTANT MISO SOUP
インスタント味噌汁

—

Wrap 1 tablespoon of your favourite miso, 1 teaspoon dried wakame, 2 g (1/16 oz) katsuobushi (dried bonito flakes) or 2 g (1/16 oz) dashi powder, and 1 finely chopped spring onion (scallion) in plastic wrap and take it with you in your lunchbox or on a picnic.

Scrape the miso mixture into a mug and pour in 200 ml (7 fl oz) hot water. Stir until the miso dissolves.

Add some ground sesame seeds. Shichimi Togarashi (see page 166) is also good to add. Serves 1.

02. PORK MISO MIX
豚味噌

—

Heat a frying pan over medium heat. Fry 250 g (9 oz) pork mince until it is just cooked through.

Mix 1/4 cup (60 ml) red miso with 2 teaspoons light brown sugar and 2 tablespoons mirin in a small bowl to create a loose paste.

Pour the paste into the pan and mix.

Turn off the heat and set the pan aside.

Keep the pork and miso mix in an airtight container and refrigerate for up to 3 days. Serves 4.

03. MISO DRESSING
味噌ドレッシング

—

Toast 1 tablespoon sesame seeds in a small frying pan over low heat. As soon as you hear the seeds popping, remove from the heat and leave to cool. Transfer the seeds to a *suribachi* or mortar and coarsely grind them.

Stir 2½ tablespoons light brown sugar, 1/4 cup (60 ml) white miso, 2 tablespoons tahini, 2¼ teaspoons soy sauce and the sesame seeds in a bowl until the sugar has dissolved.

Transfer to a screw-top jar. Add 75 ml (2¼ fl oz) sunflower oil, 2 tablespoons toasted sesame oil, 3 tablespoons rice vinegar and 1/4 cup (60 ml) water.

Shake vigorously until the dressing emulsifies. Serve on tofu, chicken salad, steamed broccoli, carrots or a leafy salad. Makes 350 ml (12 fl oz).

04. MISO WALNUT DIP
くるみ味噌

—

Preheat the oven to 170°C (340°F) and toast 100 g (3½ oz) walnuts for 10 minutes. Wrap them in a clean tea towel and scrub the skin in between your hands in the towel. Roughly chop the scrubbed walnuts.

Put 2 tablespoons white miso, 2 tablespoons light brown sugar and 2½ tablespoons mirin in a small saucepan and place over low heat. Keep stirring to a smooth paste.

Scrape the miso mixture into a bowl. Combine with the chopped walnuts. Serve with vegetable sticks or as an *onigiri* filling. Makes 1 small jar of dip.

05. HONEY-MISO MARINATED SALMON, DUCK OR CHICKEN
はちみつ味噌マリネ

—

Mix 150 g (5½ oz) red miso, 150 ml (5 fl oz) runny honey and 1 tablespoon sake in a small bowl.

Coat 4 boneless fillets of salmon, duck or chicken with the miso marinade in a resealable plastic bag. Leave in the fridge overnight or for up to 3 days. As the days go by, the flavour gets stronger.

Preheat the grill to medium–high.

Remove the fillets from the marinade and wipe off the miso marinade using paper towel.

Cook under the grill for 5–8 minutes on each side until cooked through. Serves 4.

06. MISO CARAMEL SAUCE
味噌キャラメルソース

—

Tip 125 g (4½ oz) caster (superfine) sugar into a frying pan and heat over medium–low heat. Cook until the sugar dissolves and turns a deep caramel colour. Swirl the pan, but do not stir. As soon as the sugar turns into caramel, take the pan off the heat.

Add 80 ml thick (double) cream and 25 g (1 oz) unsalted butter and mix until well combined.

Add 2 tablespoons white miso to the pan and stir until the miso dissolves.

Transfer the sauce to a screw-top jar and store in the fridge. It's great with ice cream. Makes 200 ml (7 fl oz).

YUZU KOSHO
(SALTED LIME & CHILLI PASTE)

柚子胡椒

MAKES: A 50 ML (1½ FL OZ) JAR **PREPARATION:** *20 MINUTES*

FRESH

20 g (¾ oz) grated organic unwaxed lime zest (from about 9 limes)

20 g (¾ oz) green chilli, finely chopped

PANTRY

40 g (1½ oz) sea salt flakes

Yuzu kosho is a condiment from the Kyushu district, located in the southern part of Japan. It is typically made with yuzu, an aromatic Japanese citrus fruit. However, the yuzu fruit can be difficult to find outside Japan, so I tried using limes and it worked extremely well. Try it with Sea Bream Carpaccio (see page 158) or Tea-braised Pork (see page 138).

—

Combine the grated lime zest, green chilli and sea salt in a mortar and grind until all the ingredients are incorporated.

It's best to leave the paste to stand for 1 week so that the flavour can mature. Store it in a sterilised jar in the fridge for 2 months.

SMOKY TEA &
GREEN TEA SALT

ほうじ茶塩、抹茶塩

MAKES: 15 G (½ OZ) EACH PREPARATION: 10 MINUTES

HOJICHA SALT

1 teaspoon hojicha
(Japanese smoky tea)

1 tablespoon sea salt flakes

MATCHA GREEN
TEA SALT

½ tablespoon sea salt flakes

½ tablespoon matcha powder
(green tea powder)

Hojicha gives this dish a hint of smokiness, while matcha adds a lovely subtle bitterness. This is great for Tempura (see page 122) or sprinkled on sashimi or carpaccio.

—

For the Hojicha Salt:
Finely grind the tea in a spice grinder or mortar and pestle. Add the salt and break up the bigger pieces, but keep the mixture quite coarse.

For the Matcha Green Tea Salt:
Break up the bigger pieces of salt in a spice grinder or mortar and pestle. Stir in the matcha powder.

Store both salts in separate sterilised screw-top jars for up to 2–3 months.

CRISPY GARLIC
& CHILLI OIL

ラー油

MAKES: 240ML (8 FL OZ) **PREPARATION:** *10 MINUTES* **COOKING:** *15 MINUTES*

FRESH

8 garlic cloves, sliced

4 spring onions (scallions),
    thinly sliced

PANTRY

100 ml (3½ fl oz) sunflower oil

2 tablespoons chilli flakes

100 ml (3½ fl oz) toasted sesame oil

¼ cup (35 g) peanuts,
    roughly chopped

4 teaspoons light brown sugar

1 teaspoon sea salt

Using this popular oil will elevate the flavour of a simple stir-fry, salad or fried rice to the next level. It is also great for Ramen (see page 98), Gyoza Dumplings (see page 54) or on plain silken tofu.

—

Combine the sunflower oil, chilli flakes, garlic and spring onion in a frying pan. Heat over medium–low heat to infuse the flavour of the ingredients into the oil for about 15 minutes or until the garlic becomes crisp and a light golden colour.

Remove the pan from the heat. Add the sesame oil, peanuts, sugar and salt and mix until the sugar and salt have dissolved.

Store the oil in a sterilised screw-top jar for up to 2 weeks.

FURIKAKE
(DRY SEASONING MIX)

ふりかけ

*MAKES: A 50 ML (1¾ OZ) JAR **PREPARATION:** 5 MINUTES
COOKING: 10-15 MINUTES*

PANTRY

75 g (2½ oz) katsuobushi
(dried bonito flakes)

15 kombu (dried kelp) sheets,
finely shredded

1 tablespoon soy sauce

3 tablespoons mirin

1 tablespoon white sesame seeds,
toasted

20 g (¾ oz) walnuts, roughly chopped

Furikake is a Japanese dry sprinkle, mainly served on steamed
rice (see page 208) or mixed into Onigiri (see page 114), but you
should also try it as a sprinkle on noodles or steamed vegetables.
I came up with this recipe when I was trying to find a use for the
ingredients left over from making dashi stock. Katsuobushi and
kombu can be frozen if you want to make this later.

—

Put the katsuobushi and kombu in a frying pan over low heat.
Add the soy sauce, mirin, sesame seeds and walnuts and cook
until the liquid evaporates. The mixture should be dried a little.

Store the mixture in the fridge in a sterilised screw-top jar for
up to a week.

DAIKON PICKLES
WITH LEMON

大根とレモンの漬物

SERVES: 4-5 AS A SIDE DISH **PREPARATION:** *20 MINUTES, PLUS PICKLING*

FRESH

500 g (1 lb 2 oz) daikon radish
    (peeled weight), cut into 1.5 cm
    (⅝ inch) matchsticks

juice of ½ lemon

peel from ¼ lemon, white pith
    removed, very thinly sliced

PANTRY

8 g (⅛ oz) sea salt flakes

50 ml (1½ fl oz) rice vinegar

25 g (1 oz) caster (superfine) sugar

We have many varieties of pickles in Japan and this is
one of the most popular ones. I have made it with lemon
instead of the traditional yuzu. These are lovely served
with any of the sushi in this book.

—

Place the daikon in a glass or ceramic bowl, sprinkle with the
salt and massage them together. Leave for 30 minutes, until
the liquid is released from the daikon.

Use clean hands to squeeze the daikon to remove any
excess liquid.

Mix the vinegar, sugar, lemon juice and lemon peel in a
small bowl until the sugar dissolves. Pour the pickling liquid
onto the daikon, making sure the daikon is completely covered.
Refrigerate for at least 1 hour, or overnight if you have time.

Decant the mixture into a sterilised jar, refrigerate and consume
within 4 days.

PICKLED GINGER

生姜の酢漬け

MAKES: A 350 ML (12 FL OZ) JAR **PREPARATION:** *15 MINUTES, PLUS PICKLING* **COOKING:** *5 MINUTES*

FRESH

200 g (7 oz) fresh ginger,
  peeled and thinly sliced

PANTRY

½ teaspoon sea salt,
  plus extra for salting

100 ml (3½ fl oz) rice vinegar

90 g (3¼ oz) light brown sugar

50 ml (1½ fl oz) sake

When you find fresh ginger, do try this – it's less sweet and much healthier than the commercial product. It's a perfect palate cleanser to have with any of the sushi in this book.

—

Place the ginger in a bowl and sprinkle with some salt. Set aside for 10 minutes.

Combine the salt, vinegar, sugar, sake and 50 ml (1½ fl oz) water in a small saucepan. Simmer over medium heat until the sugar and salt have dissolved.

Use clean hands to squeeze the ginger to remove any excess liquid and place the ginger in a sterilised jar. Pour the warm pickling liquid over the ginger and leave to pickle overnight.

You can eat this the next day, but it tastes better after 3 days. Keep refrigerated for up to 1 month.

QUICK SOY-PICKLED CUCUMBER & GINGER

即席きゅうりと生姜の醤油漬け

SERVES: 4 ***PREPARATION:*** *15 MINUTES, PLUS 30 MINUTES STANDING*

FRESH

1 large cucumber, about 500 g
(1 lb 2 oz)

15 g (½ oz) fresh ginger,
peeled and thinly sliced

PANTRY

2 tablespoons soy sauce

1 tablespoon rice vinegar

1 tablespoon mirin

½ teaspoon light brown sugar

This is an instant pickle that can be made in just a few minutes and added to your meal as a side dish. The crunchy texture of the cucumber and heat from the ginger makes it hard to stop eating once you start. Try it with any of the main meal dishes.

—

Partially peel the cucumber, then cut it in half horizontally. Scrape out the seeds with a teaspoon and discard. Bash the cucumber with a rolling pin to break it into bite-sized pieces (the uneven cuts help the sauce absorb quickly).

Combine the soy sauce, vinegar, mirin and sugar, then mix with the cucumber. Add the ginger and leave to stand for 30 minutes.

SENMAIZUKE (TURNIP PICKLES)

千枚漬け

SERVES: *4-5 AS A SIDE DISH* **PREPARATION:** *20 MINUTES, PLUS 8 HOURS PICKLING*

FRESH

500 g (1 lb 2 oz) turnips (peeled weight),
cut into 2 mm (1⁄16 inch) slices

PANTRY

8 g (1⁄8 oz) sea salt

2 teaspoons rice vinegar

1½ teaspoons caster (superfine) sugar

1 dried chilli, seeded and thinly sliced

4 cm (1½ inch) square piece of kombu
(dried kelp), very thinly sliced

Kyoto is famous for its quality pickles and this is one of them.
Senmai means 'a thousand slices', which is where the name
comes from. The variety called 'Tokyo turnips' are ideal, but
kohlrabi also works well. These pickles are perfect served
as an accompaniment to any main meal.

—

Place the turnips in a clean, non-metallic bowl. Add the salt,
vinegar, sugar, chilli and kombu and gently mix together.

Put a small, clean plate on top of the turnips and place a 500 g
(1 lb 2 oz) weight on top. Place in the fridge overnight.

Decant the pickles into a sterilised jar and store in the fridge
for up to 4 days.

DESSERTS
& DRINKS

ICED MATCHA
GREEN TEA LATTE

アイス抹茶ラテ

SERVES: 4 PREPARATION: 2 MINUTES

FRESH

600 ml (21 fl oz) milk

ice cubes

PANTRY

4 teaspoons light brown sugar

15 g (½ oz) matcha powder
(green tea powder),
plus extra to serve

Matcha powder itself is very strong and bitter, so you only need a small amount in this trendy drink. It's also delicious served hot and works well with plant-based milks.

—

Pour the milk into a bowl, add the sugar and mix until the sugar has dissolved.

Sift the matcha powder into a bowl. Add a small amount of the sugared milk and beat with a small whisk until combined.

Divide the rest of the sugared milk among four glasses filled with ice cubes. Pour in the whisked matcha and whisk to create a froth. Dust with some extra matcha powder to serve.

MATCHA ICE-CREAM SANDWICH

抹茶アイスのクッキーサンド

MAKES: 6 **PREPARATION:** *15 MINUTES, PLUS 4-6 HOURS FREEZING* **COOKING:** *20 MINUTES*

FRESH

6 organic egg yolks

280 ml (9½ fl oz) thick (double) cream

2¼ cups (560 ml) full-cream (whole) milk

PANTRY

⅔ cup (150 g) caster (superfine) sugar

1 vanilla pod, split lengthways and scraped to remove the seeds

2 tablespoons matcha powder (green tea powder)

12 digestive biscuits

This refreshing, subtly bitter green tea ice cream would be perfect for the end of any Japanese meal. If you're using an ice-cream maker and the bowl needs to be chilled, you can prepare this a day in advance.

—

Mix the egg yolks and sugar in a large bowl.

Combine the cream, milk, vanilla seeds and vanilla pod in a saucepan. Cook over medium–low heat until just below boiling point. Remove from the heat. Pour just one ladleful of the liquid into the egg mixture, mix well and then add the rest of the milk. Mix completely to dissolve the sugar.

Rinse the saucepan and pour the egg and milk mixture back into the pan. Cook over medium–low heat, stirring constantly, until the custard is thick enough to coat the back of a spoon.

Remove the vanilla pod and scrape the custard into a bowl. Sift the matcha powder over the custard and carefully stir to remove all of the lumps. Cover with plastic wrap until cooled.

Pour the cooled custard into an ice-cream maker and churn according to the machine's instructions. Alternatively, pour the custard into a container to freeze for 2–3 hours. Whisk the custard, then return to the freezer and repeat this process for the next 2–3 hours, until frozen.

To serve, scoop about 90 g (3¼ oz) of the ice cream and sandwich it between two digestive biscuits. You can freeze the sandwiches again to serve later if you wish.

SHAVED ICE WITH FRESH FRUIT PURÉE

かき氷

SERVES: 4 PREPARATION: 20 MINUTES, PLUS FREEZING

FRESH

40 ice cubes, about 900 g (2 lb)

200 g (7 oz) frozen strawberries

100 g (3½ oz) fresh or tinned lychees, frozen

150 g (5½ oz) frozen mango

½ cup (125 ml) filtered water

juice and grated zest of ½ unwaxed organic lime

diced fresh strawberries, to serve

diced fresh mango, to serve

Tip: For best results, use store-bought ice cubes or make ice cubes with mineral water or boiled and cooled water.

The Japanese feel as if summer has arrived when shaved ice is added to the menu of Japanese sweet shops. It's time-consuming to make, but if you crush the ice in a food processor and freeze it again, you can process the ice again just before you eat it. This will also give much better results – it's like eating fluffy, powdery snow.

—

If you are blitzing the ice twice, place the ice cubes in a food processor and blitz until you get snowy ice. Quickly tip it into a deep container (try not to compress the ice flakes) and keep this in the freezer for at least 2 hours.

Tip the frozen strawberries and lychees into a blender. Blend to a smooth purée, then transfer to a bowl and rinse the blender.

Tip the frozen mango and water into the blender. Blend to a smooth purée. Add the lime juice and zest.

Transfer the ice flakes to a food processor and blitz until you get powdery ice.

Divide the shaved ice among four bowls, forming a mound in the centre of each without compressing the ice. Pour the two kinds of fruit purée over the ice and decorate with fresh fruit. Serve immediately.

Tip: When the fruits are not in season and not naturally sweet enough, you can add a little icing (confectioners') sugar to the fruit purées, to taste.

SWEET TOFU WITH HOJICHA SYRUP

杏仁豆腐とほうじ茶のシロップ

SERVES: 4 PREPARATION: 20 MINUTES COOKING: 5 MINUTES

FRESH

400 ml (14 fl oz) full-cream (whole) milk

200 ml (7 fl oz) hot filtered water

8 strawberries, sliced

PANTRY

4 gelatine sheets

1 teaspoon almond extract

8 g (⅛ oz) hojicha tea leaves (smoky roasted tea)

80 g (2¾ oz) caster (superfine) sugar

This milk jelly looks similar to tofu, hence the name 'Sweet Tofu'. It's usually served with a plain sugar syrup, but adding the hojicha gives a pleasant hint of smokiness and a subtle caramel flavour.

—

Place the gelatine sheets in a bowl of water and leave to soak for 10 minutes.

Pour the milk into a small saucepan and set it over medium heat to warm the milk. Remove from the heat and stir in the almond extract.

Remove the gelatine sheets from the water. Squeeze them to remove any excess water, then add them to the milk and mix until they are completely dissolved.

Line the base and sides of a shallow tray with plastic wrap and pour the milk mixture into the tray. Cover with plastic wrap and place in the fridge for at least 2 hours to set.

Pour the hot water over the tea leaves and leave to steep for 2 minutes, then strain through a tea strainer.

Place the sugar and tea in a small saucepan over medium heat and cook until syrupy. Remove from the heat and leave it to cool, then chill in the fridge.

Divide the milk jelly and strawberries among four bowls. Pour the syrup over the top to serve.

SHIRATAMA MOCHI BALLS WITH BROWN SUGAR & GINGER SYRUP

白玉だんごと生姜黒蜜

SERVES: 4 PREPARATION: 20 MINUTES COOKING: 10 MINUTES

FRESH

15 g (½ oz) fresh ginger,
  peeled and thinly sliced

PANTRY

80 g (2¾ oz) dark brown sugar

100 g (3½ oz) glutinous rice flour

2 tablespoons kinako (soybean
  powder) or salted peanut powder
  (blitz salted peanuts in a mini
  food processor), to serve

vanilla ice cream and fresh fruit
  such as sliced oranges, to serve

This silky *shiratama mochi* is made with glutinous rice flour, which can be found in any large supermarket, Asian grocery store or online. It's a quick and easy dessert to prepare and you can even freeze it when it is uncooked and boil it later when you need it.

—

To make the syrup, put the sugar, 200 ml (7 fl oz) water and the ginger in a small saucepan. Cook over medium heat until it has a thick and syrupy consistency. Set aside.

To make the mochi balls, sift the glutinous rice flour into a bowl. Add 30 ml (1 fl oz) water at first and mix with your hands. Add another 70 ml (2¼ fl oz) water, a little at a time, until the mixture comes together into a dough and is not sticking to your fingers or the bowl. You may not need all of the water. If you add too much, add a little more flour to achieve the right consistency.

Cut the dough in half and roll into two 2.5 cm (1 inch) thick logs. Cut each log into 12 equal discs so that you have 24 slices. Roll each disc into a ball, then flatten it to about 1.5 cm (⅝ inch) thick and make a dent in the middle with your index finger. Prepare a large bowl with plenty of iced water.

Bring a saucepan with plenty of water to the boil over high heat. Drop the mochi balls in all at once, stirring gently to prevent them from sticking to the base of the pan. Once the balls float back to the surface, cook for another minute.

Scoop out the balls with a slotted spoon and drop into the iced water. When the mochi have cooled, divide them among four bowls. Spoon the syrup over the top and serve with the kinako or peanut powder, ice cream and fresh fruit.

CARAMELISED SWEET POTATO & BLACK SESAME

大学芋

SERVES: 4 PREPARATION: 10 MINUTES COOKING: 20 MINUTES

FRESH

500 g (1 lb 2 oz) sweet potatoes,
    cut into wedges

PANTRY

700 ml (24 fl oz) sunflower oil,
    for deep-frying

60 g (2¼ oz) caster (superfine) sugar

2 tablespoons honey

1 tablespoon black sesame seeds

Sweet potato is often used in desserts as well as in savoury dishes in Japan. If you can find red-skinned, yellow/white fleshed sweet potatoes or purple sweet potatoes, these will produce the best results.

—

Heat the sunflower oil in a deep saucepan over medium–high heat to 160°C (320°F) and fry the sweet potatoes for 3–4 minutes, until soft when poked. Lift them out with a metal strainer and drain on paper towel.

Heat the oil to 180°C (350°F) and fry the sweet potatoes again, until they turn a golden colour. Lift them out with a metal strainer and drain on fresh paper towel.

Combine the sugar, honey and 2 tablespoons water in a frying pan over medium heat. Cook until the sugar has melted and turned a deep golden colour.

Add the sweet potatoes to the pan and mix with the caramel. Take the pan off the heat, sprinkle the sweet potatoes with the black sesame seeds and serve.

NASHI PEAR, SAKE & SHISO FROZEN COCKTAIL

梨、紫蘇、酒のフローズンカクテル

SERVES: 4 **PREPARATION:** *15 MINUTES, PLUS 3 HOURS FREEZING* **COOKING:** *10 MINUTES*

FRESH

2 nashi pears, about 500 g (1 lb 2 oz), peeled and cored

4 shiso (perilla) leaves or small mint leaves, plus extra to garnish

PANTRY

70 g (2½ oz) caster (superfine) sugar

160 ml (5¼ fl oz) sake

This is a super-refreshing drink that is perfect for summer afternoons. A nashi pear (or Asian pear) looks like a pale-yellow apple. Although it is called a pear, the taste and texture are quite different from European pears. It has a high water content and is fresh, crisp and juicy, with a beautiful aroma.

—

Mix the sugar with 70 ml (2¼ fl oz) water in a small saucepan over medium heat and bring to the boil. Reduce the heat and simmer until thickened and syrupy. Remove from the heat and set aside to cool.

Put four small glasses in the fridge until you are ready to serve the cocktail.

Put the pear flesh in a blender and blend until it is smooth. Add ½ cup (125 ml) of the cooled syrup and the sake. Pour into an airtight container and transfer to the freezer for about 3 hours, until the mixture has a slushy consistency.

When the pear mixture has reached the desired consistency, remove it from the freezer. Blend in the shiso or mint leaves and pour into the chilled glasses. Garnish with extra shiso or mint to serve.

BASICS

BASIC DASHI STOCK

基本の出汁

MAKES: ABOUT 800 ML (28 FL OZ) **PREPARATION:** *5 MINUTES, PLUS SOAKING*
COOKING: *15 MINUTES*

PANTRY

10 g (¼ oz) kombu (dried kelp)

4 cups (1 litre) filtered water

10 g (¼ oz) katsuobushi
(dried bonito flakes) – large
flakes are preferable for dashi

This is the foundation for many Japanese recipes. Of course, you can easily buy good-quality dashi powder nowadays, and it's instant. However, please try making dashi from scratch. It is actually very easy when you have all of the ingredients handy. There is also an option to make a second dashi stock to recycle the leftovers from the first dashi, which will be suitable for stronger-flavoured dishes, such as miso soup and stew.

—

FOR THE FIRST DASHI STOCK:

01. Soak the kombu in the filtered water, covered with plastic wrap, for at least 30 minutes or overnight in the fridge.

02. Pour the kombu and water into a saucepan set over medium–low heat and slowly bring it to just below boiling – this will take about 10 minutes. Remove the kombu – keep it for the second dashi stock or to make Furikake (see page 176).

03. Bring the kombu stock to the boil. As soon as it has boiled, take it off the heat and add the katsuobushi. Return the pan to low heat and cook for 4 minutes.

04. Line a fine strainer with paper towel and place it over a large bowl. Pour the stock through the strainer. Your first dashi stock is now ready.

FOR THE SECOND DASHI STOCK (OPTIONAL):

01. Combine the kombu and katsuobushi in a saucepan with 2 cups (500 ml) water. Bring to the boil, then reduce the heat and simmer for 10 minutes. Add 10 g (¼ oz) fresh katsuobushi. Turn off the heat and leave for 5 minutes, then drain through a strainer lined with paper towel.

02. Discard the katsuobushi and kombu or recycle and make Furikake (see page 176). The dashi can be kept in the fridge for 3 days or can be frozen and used within 1 month.

KOMBU (KELP) DASHI STOCK

昆布出汁

MAKES: 900 ML (31 FL OZ) *PREPARATION:* 5 MINUTES, PLUS 3-8 HOURS SOAKING
COOKING: 10 MINUTES

PANTRY

4 cups (1 litre) filtered water

10 g (¼ oz) kombu (dried kelp)

This is a vegetarian version of dashi stock. It can also be mixed with Shiitake Mushroom Dashi Stock (see opposite), if you like.

—

Pour the filtered water into a bowl. Add the kombu and soak, covered with plastic wrap, for at least 3 hours or overnight.

Pour the kombu and water into a saucepan over medium–low heat. Heat until just below boiling point (this will take about 10 minutes). Remove the kombu.

Discard the kombu or save it to make Furikake (see page 176) – it can be frozen, too.

The dashi can be kept in the fridge for 3 days or can be frozen and used within 1 month.

DRIED SHIITAKE MUSHROOM DASHI STOCK

干し椎茸の出汁

MAKES: 900 ML (31 FL OZ)   *PREPARATION: 5 MINUTES, PLUS 8 HOURS SOAKING*

PANTRY

4 cups (1 litre) filtered water

30 g (1 oz) dried shiitake mushrooms

This, along with the Kombu Dashi Stock (see opposite), is a great vegetarian stock option. Dried shiitake provides such a powerful flavour and it has a nice sweetness. This is suitable for stronger-flavoured dishes like stews or noodle broths.

—

Pour the filtered water into a bowl, add the dried shiitake and leave to soak and infuse overnight in the fridge.

Strain the dashi. Discard the shiitake, or use it for Chirashi Sushi (see page 146).

The dashi can be kept in the fridge for 3 days or can be frozen and used within 1 month.

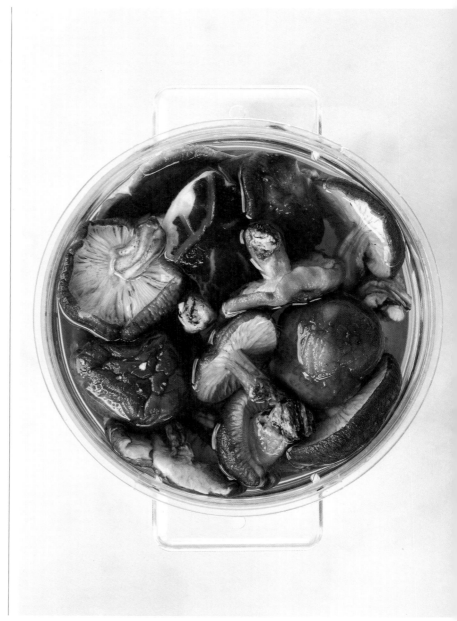

— HOW TO MAKE —
STEAMED RICE

白米

SERVES: 4 **PREPARATION:** *5 MINUTES, PLUS 30-60 MINUTES DRAINING* **COOKING:** *15 MINUTES*

PANTRY

300 g (10½ oz) Japanese rice

The general rule of rice to water ratio is 15 per cent more water than rice by weight. There are so many varieties of Japanese rice available – some types are expensive but worth a try. For example, newly harvested rice has a truly sublime flavour, and if you ever find *sinmai*, which means 'new rice', please try it – you will be surprised at how amazing it is!

—

01. Place the rice in a fine strainer and set over a bowl filled with cold water. Gently stir and wash the rice with your hands. As soon as the water turns milky, lift the strainer and drain the water. Repeat this process three to four times until the water is less milky. Leave the rice in the strainer to drain for 30–60 minutes. The rice should turn clear to white during this process.

02. Place the drained rice in a heavy-based saucepan (ideally cast-iron) with 350 ml (12 fl oz) water. Cover the pan with a heavy, tight-fitting lid.

03. Bring the rice to the boil over high heat. As soon as you can hear the water boiling vigorously and can see liquid bubbling up from the pan, reduce the heat and cook for 11 minutes. While cooking the rice, do not lift the lid – this is a strict rule!

04. Remove the pan from the heat and leave to stand, covered, for 10 minutes.

05. Open the lid and gently fluff the rice with a rice paddle.

SUSHI RICE

すし飯

SERVES: 3-4 **PREPARATION:** *20 MINUTES, PLUS 30-60 MINUTES STANDING* **COOKING:** *20 MINUTES*

PANTRY

300 g (10½ oz) Japanese rice

50 ml (1½ fl oz) rice vinegar

1½ tablespoons caster (superfine) sugar

1 teaspoon sea salt

You want the rice to retain the whole grain and not get mashed for sushi rice, so be mindful of that when you are mixing the rice with the paddle. It's a good idea to get someone to help you as it's hard to fan and mix the rice at the same time.

—

Place the rice in a fine strainer and set over a bowl filled with cold water. Gently stir and wash the rice with your hands. As soon as the water turns milky, lift the strainer and drain the water. Repeat this process three to four times until the water is less milky. Leave the rice in the strainer to drain for 30–60 minutes. The rice should turn clear to white during this process.

Place the rice in a heavy-based saucepan (ideally cast-iron) with 1⅓ cups (330 ml) water and cover with a heavy, tight-fitting lid. Bring the rice to the boil over high heat. As soon as you hear the water boiling vigorously and see liquid bubbling up from the pan, reduce the heat to low and cook for 11 minutes. While cooking the rice, do not lift the lid – this is a strict rule! Remove the pan from the heat and leave to stand, covered, for 10 minutes.

Mix the rice vinegar, sugar and salt in a small bowl and stir until the sugar has dissolved.

Open the lid of the pan and gently fluff the rice with a moistened rice paddle or spatula. Transfer the rice to a tray and pour the sushi vinegar over the rice. Mix with rice paddles as if you are cutting the rice to get rid of the lumps, but try not to mash the rice.

Once the rice and sushi vinegar are mixed together, fan and toss the rice to cool it. Cool until the rice comes to room temperature.

Cover the rice with a clean, wet tea towel. It's best to use the rice while it is still slightly warm. If you are not using it immediately, leave it at room temperature – do not keep it in the fridge as the rice will harden.

MENTSUYU (NOODLE SAUCE)

めんつゆ

MAKES: 2 CUPS (500 ML) **PREPARATION:** *10 MINUTES, PLUS 8 HOURS STANDING* **COOKING:** *5 MINUTES*

PANTRY

1 cup (250 ml) soy sauce

1 cup (250 ml) mirin

½ cup (125 ml) sake

1 tablespoon light brown sugar

7 cm (2¾ inch) square piece of kombu (dried kelp)

15 g (½ oz) katsuobushi (dried bonito flakes)

2 dried shiitake mushrooms

This is a concentrated noodle sauce that you can dilute with cold or hot water. It is so versatile – it can also be added to oil to make an amazing salad dressing, used as a flavouring for a stewed dish or even as a dipping sauce for tempura. This sauce will give your cooking an instant Japanese flair. It can be used in place of dashi stock in most recipes.

—

Put all the ingredients into a saucepan and bring to the boil, then immediately remove from the heat. Set aside to cool and keep in the fridge overnight.

Strain the sauce through a fine strainer and discard the kombu, katsuobushi and shiitake mushrooms.

Pour the sauce into a screw-top jar and keep in the fridge for up to a month.

QUICK TONKATSU SAUCE

トンカツソース

MAKES: *ABOUT ½ CUP (125 ML)* **PREPARATION:** *10 MINUTES*

FRESH

½ teaspoon freshly squeezed
  lemon juice

PANTRY

2 tablespoons tomato sauce (ketchup)

¼ cup (60 ml) Worcestershire sauce

2 teaspoons dijon mustard

4 teaspoons soy sauce

¼ cup (45 g) light brown sugar

a pinch of sea salt

¼ cup (40 g) white sesame seeds,
  toasted, optional

Tonkatsu sauce is the Japanese equivalent to British brown sauce. You will find ready-made tonkatsu sauce in any Japanese grocery store, Asian food store or online. However, it's not too difficult to make from scratch. Here is my quick, easy-to-prepare version. Try it with Okonomiyaki (see page 46) or Kushikatsu (see page 142).

—

Mix the tomato sauce, Worcestershire sauce, mustard, soy sauce, sugar, lemon juice and salt in a bowl until well combined.

If you are making this to store, don't add the sesame seeds at this stage. Store the sauce in the fridge in a clean, screw-top jar for up to a month.

Place the toasted sesame seeds in a *suribachi* or mortar and coarsely grind. Mix them into the sauce just before serving.

PONZU

ポン酢

MAKES: 1½ CUPS (375 ML) *PREPARATION:* 15 MINUTES, PLUS 8 HOURS RESTING *COOKING:* 5 MINUTES

FRESH

4 teaspoons freshly squeezed
lemon juice

140 ml (4½ fl oz) freshly squeezed
orange juice

PANTRY

½ cup (125 ml) soy sauce

½ cup (125 ml) mirin

¼ cup (60 ml) sake

10 g (¼ oz) dried shiitake mushrooms

10 g (¼ oz) katsuobushi (dried
bonito flakes)

Ponzu combines dashi ingredients (such as katsuobushi and dried shiitake) and infused soy sauce with citrus fruit. It's great with grilled meat, with sashimi or carpaccio, as a dipping sauce for Hotpot (see page 136) and Gyoza Dumplings (see page 54), and as a salad dressing.

—

Mix the soy sauce, mirin and sake in a saucepan and heat until just below boiling point. Add the shiitake and katsuobushi and transfer it to the fridge to rest overnight.

Strain the sauce mixture into a bowl and discard the katsuobushi. Keep the shiitake to re-use in another recipe.

Strain the lemon and orange juices and add to the soy mixture.

TERIYAKI SAUCE

照り焼きソース

SERVES: ABOUT 225 ML (7½ FL OZ) **PREPARATION:** *5 MINUTES* **COOKING:** *5 MINUTES*

FRESH

1 cm (½ inch) piece of fresh ginger,
    peeled and thinly sliced

1 spring onion (scallion),
    cut into thirds

PANTRY

150 ml (5 fl oz) soy sauce

100 ml (3½ fl oz) mirin

50 ml (1½ fl oz) sake

5 tablespoons light brown sugar

This sweet and salty soy sauce is one of the most popular
Japanese cooking sauces. It's used not only for Teriyaki
Chicken (see page 90) but also for Yakitori (see page 48).
It's great cooked with salmon or in a vegetable stir-fry.

—

Place all the ingredients in a small saucepan and bring to the boil
over medium heat. As soon as the sauce starts to boil, reduce the
heat and simmer for 5 minutes, or until the sauce has slightly
thickened. Take the pan off the heat and leave it to cool.

Remove and discard the ginger and spring onion. Pour the sauce
into a sterilised jar and keep in the fridge for up to 1 month.

— MENU PLANNER —

JAPANESE-STYLE BREAKFAST Ochazuke (see page 50) / Quick Soy-pickled Cucumber & Ginger (see page 182) / Nametake (see page 164) / Hot Spring Poached Eggs (see page 76) / Miso Soup (see page 82)

TEMAKI DIY SUSHI PARTY Temaki Sushi (see page 130) / Egg Crepes (see page 76) / Pickled Ginger (see page 180) / Onion & Fennel Salad (see page 80) / Sake-steamed Clams (see page 84)

OHANAMI (CHERRY BLOSSOM ADMIRING PARTY) Onigiri (see page 114) / Inari Sushi (see page 134) / Japanese-style Potato salad (see page 28) / Soy-marinated Boiled Eggs (see page 76) / Daikon Pickles with Lemon (see page 178)

RAMEN FEAST Ramen (see page 98) / Gyoza Dumplings (see page 54) / Karaage (see page 42) / Crispy Garlic & Chilli Oil (see page 174) / Ponzu (see page 216)

CASUAL EVENING DRINKS, IZAKAYA STYLE Nashi Pear, Sake & Shiso Frozen Cocktail (see page 200) / Tuna Tataki (see page 44) / Lotus Root Crisps (see page 30) / Grilled Padrón Peppers (see page 40) / Matcha Ice-cream Sandwich (see page 190)

BARBECUE Yakitori (see page 48) / Grilled Padrón Peppers (see page 40) / Grilled Eggplant with Ginger (see page 62) / Tofu, Tomato & Shiso Salad (see page 68) / Miso Caramel Sauce served with Vanilla Ice Cream (see page 168)

VEGETARIAN SPREAD Nasu Dengaku (see page 38) / Homemade Sesame Tofu (see page 70) / Grilled Shiitake Mushrooms with Garlic Butter (see page 32) / Ganmodoki (see page 26) / Sweet Tofu with Hojicha Syrup (see page 194)

WEEKEND DINNER WITH FAMILY Hotpot (see page 136) / Green Beans with Sesame Dressing (see page 66) / Steamed Rice (see page 208) / Japanese Egg Drop Soup (see page 76) / Senmaizuke (see page 184)

INDEX

Published in 2020 by Murdoch Books,
an imprint of Allen & Unwin
First published in 2018 by Hachette Livre (Marabout)

Murdoch Books Australia
83 Alexander Street
Crows Nest NSW 2065
Phone: +61 (0) 2 8425 0100
murdochbooks.com.au
info@murdochbooks.com.au

Murdoch Books UK
Ormond House, 26–27 Boswell Street
London WC1N 3JZ
Phone: +44 (0) 20 8785 5995
murdochbooks.co.uk
info@murdochbooks.co.uk

For corporate orders & custom publishing,
contact our business development team at
salesenquiries@murdochbooks.com.au

Publisher: Corinne Roberts
English-language editor: Justine Harding
Photographer: Lisa Linder
Internal design & illustration: Michelle Tilly
Cover design: Estee Sarsfield
Production director: Lou Playfair

Text © 2018 Marabout
The moral rights of the author have been asserted.

ISBN 978 1 76052 562 0 Australia
ISBN 978 1 91163 277 1 UK

A catalogue record for this book
is available from the National
Library of Australia

A catalogue record for this book is available
from the British Library

Printed and bound in China by 1010 Printing
International Limited

10 9 8 7 6 5 4

The paper in this book is FSC® certified.
FSC® promotes environmentally responsible,
socially beneficial and economically viable
management of the world's forests.

ACKNOWLEDGEMENTS

Firstly, huge gratitude to Catie Ziller for giving me this
great opportunity and for making this book happen.
Also thank you for guiding the team to the right path.

Thank you my dear adventure fellow, Lisa Linder. Your
endless energy and creativity always inspires me.

Giovanna – thank you for assisting, being so disciplined
and organised. Your positive energy provided us with
the most relaxed work environment. And thank you for
letting us use your beautiful kitchen as a studio.
Also thank you to the Torrico family, Salvatore, Mario,
Andrea and Luca (and their computer-game friends
who always made us laugh) for accommodating the
'chaos' we brought into your house.

Michelle Tilly – thank you for your beautiful designs
and charming illustrations, and embracing countless
design changes we requested. Also for having us at
your lovely studio in Brighton.

Abi Waters – for expert editing, coping with all the
last-minute requests and making my recipes sound
clear and easy to follow.

Charlotte, Nicola, Jess and Shambala – thank you for
being very patient recipe testers, and being the best
company in my tiny kitchen.

Tai – thank you for being my best food taster / most
positive recipe critic, and also being my personal
editor. I really couldn't have completed this project
without your encouragement.

Finally, I couldn't have done this without the support
and advice of my friends and family. My dad taught me
to appreciate how important good-quality ingredients
are. My mum and grandma taught me how to nourish
family in a busy lifestyle and taught me the best home-
style Japanese cooking.